So, You Want to Be an Internal Audit Rock Star?

Leadership Competencies to Help You Thrive!

SHANE M. ROGERS, FCA, MBA

SO, YOU WANT TO BE AN INTERNAL AUDIT ROCK STAR?
LEADERSHIP COMPETENCIES TO HELP YOU THRIVE

Published by:
Sarwil Publishing

Ebook ISBN: 9798994909812
Paperback ISBN: 9798994909805

Dedication

This book is dedicated to my wife, my four children, and my parents. I want to thank my family for all their support in writing this book, and for putting up with me as I grappled with the form and flow of this work.

More broadly, I dedicate this book to all the professionals who diligently provide Internal Audit and assurance services to corporations around the globe. The importance of objective internal audits is frequently underestimated, even though Internal Auditors consistently highlight major risks for management and boards to consider and address.

Special thanks to all those professional accountants, auditors, and managers I have worked with and learned from over many years in New York, London, Dublin, and Zurich. Your voices of reason and logic are powerful forces for good organizational stewardship and risk governance.

Finally, special thanks also to those in my network who encouraged me to write this book and who provided feedback on my draft manuscript or chapters along the way: Jamie Wylie (teacher extraordinaire), Ron Hamilton, Doug Davis, Erica McManaman, Robert Viviani, Carwyn Jones, Nick Preston, David Powell, Puneet Nagpal, Nigyar Mamedova, Jeremy Brown, Tonya Samuels, Dan Pinna, Warren Hunt, and the guitar maestro, Dennis Dawson. Your candor and feedback have been valuable and greatly appreciated, and without your collective support, I would never have been able to complete this book.

Table of Contents

INTRODUCTION

Internal Audit leaders play several critical roles in modern organizations: challengers in chief, influencers in chief, integrity demonstrators in chief, empathizers in chief, trusted sparring partners, value delivery chiefs, and catalysts in chief, among others. With unfettered access to organizational activities, systems, and resources, internal auditors occupy a unique place in the modern organization and have great expectations placed upon them.

To realize and indeed exceed these expectations, Internal Audit Leaders must lead effectively, must be trusted, and excel in all aspects of communication with management and the Board/Audit Committee. Internal Audit leadership is an art, not a science, and despite the great progress achieved through data analytics, full data hypothesis testing and more recently, artificial intelligence, it remains largely a human-to-human endeavor. I wrote this book to draw upon and share my many years of Internal Audit leadership in global investment banking and insurance businesses, and to highlight critical leadership competencies. I share insightful analogies and anecdotes from the world of rock music that internal auditors can reflect upon and be inspired by, to become more effective, creative Internal Audit leaders. Sharing my experiences, perspectives, and ideas outlined in this book is part of my giving back to the global Internal Audit community.

As a Chartered Accountant with many years of global experience, I have worked with many fantastic people in several multinational organizations and learned so much along my journey. My experiences have held me in good standing, including my journey from Staff Auditor to Chief Audit Executive, along with my successes and failures, which I hope will help Internal Auditors achieve greater impact while enjoying the process.

The role of the Internal Auditor can be a complex one in organizations these days. Internal Audit as a function has no direct operational or production role in the business per se, but at its core, its role is to help the business thrive. As assessors of risk, process understanding, internal controls design, and operational effectiveness, Internal Auditors cover a lot of ground in the modern enterprise.

Grounded in being independent, objective, and trusted advisors[1], Internal Audit plays a critical role in helping the Board, the Audit Committee, and Executive Management fulfill their stewardship responsibilities over key risks, including financial, operational, and reputational risks. The advent of full data audits and analytics, and emerging artificial intelligence tools and capabilities, is transforming modern business practices and internal auditing. Internal Auditors will need to adapt, and adapt quickly, to remain relevant.

1 Chambers, Richard F. Trusted Advisors: Key Attributes of Outstanding Internal Auditors, 2nd ed. Hoboken, NJ: Wiley, 2019.

Critical thinking, problem-solving, and structured learning abound in Internal Audit teams, and I am always amazed at how much and how quickly Internal Auditors learn. Despite this, many Internal Auditors yearn for more impact. Their alter egos have them wowing the Board with invaluable forward-looking assurance and insights. But, alas, their reality is often quite different.

Holier-than-thou opinions, verbose and confusing reports, and an excessive focus on independence cloud stakeholder perceptions of Internal Audit reality. We need to lighten our load and free up our objective voices to take our roles to another level. Just like Spinal Tap in their famous rockumentary, *This is Spinal Tap*[2], our Internal Audit amplifiers need to go to eleven when we have something special to say.

Becoming an accountant and auditor was my chosen path from a relatively early age. I was always interested in business, trends, financial results, and deals. We had some great business teachers in Terenure College, Dublin, where I attended high school. Frank Gallen was my business and accounting teacher. Back in the mid-eighties, we discussed leveraged buyouts, overtrading, and asset stripping, topics I found far more interesting than the routine debits and credits that accounting offered in abundance.

Mr. Doherty was my economics teacher, and he shared great worldly wisdom as we debated different economic models, macro and micro topics, supply-siders, and the velocity of money, to name a few areas. Back in those days, Ireland Inc. was in fairly dire straits, with massive unemployment and much old-world thinking and corruption in political circles.

2 *This is Spinal Tap* – 1984 mockumentary film written by Christopher Guest, Michael McKean, Harry Shearer and Rob Reiner.

It was not until the early nineties that Ireland Inc. got its game plan together and the Celtic Tiger Economy[3] was born in earnest. Ireland produced an abundance of Chartered Accountants, and while I cannot prove it, I do believe that the collective impact of smart, well-educated accountants played some role in helping Ireland find its place on the global stage economically. As accountants, we support good strategic decision-making and sound corporate governance practices.

These days, Ireland is among the role models for a small open economy that clearly boxes above its weight globally and is among the richest countries in Gross Domestic Product per capita. Becoming a Chartered Accountant while training at Price Waterhouse Dublin from late 1989 through mid-1993 was one of the best decisions I ever made, and it afforded me wonderful global opportunities. Moving full-time to the United States in 1993, I never looked back.

Growing up in the eighties, rock music and MTV were staples that influenced my views of the world, like many others. The music that you grow up with tends to stay with you; what you like as a teenager tends to be your go-to music for the rest of your life. That is true for me. Blues rock and heavy metal are my music genres of choice. The seventies through the nineties certainly did not disappoint in that sense.

Unusually for someone who grew up in Dublin, Ireland, Foghat, a somewhat unheard-of band in Ireland that hailed from the United Kingdom, was among my favorite artists, alongside Black Sabbath, Judas Priest, David Bowie, Motörhead, and Dio. No U2 or Simple Minds for me.

I found Foghat's music inspiring and uplifting. Their fast-paced, electric boogie blues and slide guitar always put me in a good

3 'Celtic Tiger' – a nickname for Ireland during its boom years between 1995 and 2007 when the Irish economy was growing rapidly. The Irish economy grew at an average annual rate of 9.4% between 1995 and 2000.

mood, and they could deliver the goods live. Equally, there is something in their story that evokes the underdog, fighting for survival and ultimately thriving. Sometimes that is how internal auditors feel. I know I felt that way at times in terms of handling management pushback when we identified important issues. Handling difficult situations calmly and offering solutions to management helped me through many tough audits.

In the early eighties, a friend of mine, Terrence O'Malley, picked up a copy of the Foghat Live album, recorded in 1977. We listened to it constantly. We marveled at how fast their drummer, Roger Earl, played Slow Ride[4], and at the band's perfect timing during live performances. It is a must-listen even today if you want to hear a tight rock band live, and Roger Earl and a new incarnation of Foghat musicians are still packing out theaters.

A British blues rock band, ironically, they found themselves shut out of the UK market given the malevolent influence of their former Savoy Brown manager, who made it impossible for them to get work on the UK circuit.[5] This was his payback for their desertion from the band he was managing, Savoy Brown. Savoy Brown was a successful British blues band from the mid-sixties to the early seventies. Three of the four Foghat founding members had been in the band until 1970, but decided to forge their own path.

Reduced to outsiders looking in, to their home UK market, in 1971, 'Lonesome' Dave Peverett, Roger Earl, Tony Stevens, and Rod Price formed Foghat and headed to the US, and the rest is history.[6]

---

4 Foghat *Slow Ride* – released by Bearsville records in 1975, written by Dave Peverett, produced by Nick Jameson.

5 Joe Miller, Defender of the Faith, "Roger Earl (Foghat) Interview," November 17,2023, https://defendersofthefaithmetal.com/roger-earl-foghat-interview/

6 Joe Miller, Defender of the Faith, "Roger Earl (Foghat) Interview," November 17,2023, https://defendersofthefaithmetal.com/roger-earl-foghat-interview/

Resilient to their core, Foghat overcame significant obstacles in the early seventies in their home country and rose to the challenge and kept fighting, eventually finding a way to make it happen in the United States. By 1978, they were among the biggest music acts touring the US, selling out arenas and stadiums to full capacity. The band's fortunes changed for the worse in the 1980s as they pivoted towards New Wave and lost much of their following. They did reform in the 1990s and focused on their original boogie blues rock sound and are still touring and doing well today.

Some people believe Foghat inspired the spoof rockumentary movie *This is Spinal Tap*, featuring a band of British guys touring the US trying to revive their past success, a drummer who literally blows up, and all with droll personalities. Legend has it that when the movie was released, Foghat accused the producers of *This is Spinal Tap* of secretly taping their tour bus, given the perceived alignment of rockumentary situations to actual events on the road. Who knows what really transpired? Foghat for sure, was not the only rock band to experience some 'Spinal Tap' moments on tour.

As a band, they gave back too. Famously, in 1977 they held a charity concert in *New York City, Foghat: A Blues Tribute*[7], to raise money to save the blues record collection at the New York Public Library. Foghat were joined by many great blues artists performing alongside them, including Muddy Waters, John Lee Hooker, Eddie 'Bluesman' Kirkland, Otis Blackwell, Johnny Winter, and Paul Butterfield to raise the funds required.

For the record, with Foghat as his backing band, Eddie 'Bluesman' Kirkland stole the show with various acrobatic maneuvers,

---

7 *Foghat, A Blues Tribute* – recorded in New York City at the Palladium Theatre in 1977 as a benefit concert to save the blues record collection at The New York Public Library. Performers included: Foghat, Eddie 'Bluesman' Kirkland, John Lee Hooker, Muddy Waters, Paul Butterfield, Johnny Winter, Otis Blackwell, Dave 'Honeyboy' Edwards.

including a backward tumble while playing guitar and playing the guitar behind his back.

There is no better band of musicians to help save the New York Library's blues collection than the ensemble of superstars mentioned above.

Another musical inspiration for me is Ian Fraser 'Lemmy' Kilmister (1945–2015). Lemmy was many things to many people: legend, hero, scoundrel, reprobate. He was the frontman of the heavy metal band Motörhead, a world-renowned bass guitar player and singer (or gravelly shouter might be a better description).

Surprisingly, beyond his music, the one trait everyone who knew Lemmy consistently mentions is his honesty. He was direct, blunt, and often said unpopular things. He never claimed to be perfect and was very open about his rock-and-roll lifestyle. He had his vices and demons, like we all do. However, if you watch documentaries about his life, Lemmy: The Movie[8], and his many interviews, above all else, it is his honesty that comes across loud and clear.

Despite his menacing look, he was very humble and down to earth. Lemmy never refused to sign an autograph or take a picture with a fan. He was well-read, had opinions, and was a trivia expert. His own father abandoned him and his mother when he was young, and he acknowledged that he was not fully present for his own son until much later in life. Despite this, he became a father figure to many young aspiring rock musicians.

Lemmy treated his road crew like family, and many of this team worked with him and his band for decades as they toured the world almost non-stop. You could not judge his book by its cover. He was tough and gruff, but his honesty shone through.

---

8 *Lemmy the Movie* – A documentary film which celebrates the life and rock 'n' roll philosophy of Motörhead frontman and bassist Lemmy. Directed by Wes Orshoski and Greg Oliver, released on January 13, 2011, and distributed by Lionsgate Canada.

When Lemmy died in late 2015, hundreds of thousands of people attended his funeral service virtually. World-renowned musicians, including band members from The Foo Fighters, Metallica, and Judas Priest, all eulogized his music, his life, his friendship, and particularly his honesty. My sense is that if Lemmy were in management or Internal Audit, he would have been brutally honest. He never dressed things up; he did not care whether you liked him or not. He was humble and the epitome of the term 'open, honest, and candid.'

I will mention this term several times in this book, as it is 'a call to action' for Internal Auditors to keep at the forefront of their thinking. It is no surprise then that Motörhead, despite little radio or MTV play, remained one of the most influential and respected heavy metal bands in the world for decades. In this respect, many of us could learn lessons from Lemmy and his bandmates.

In a similar vein, we as Internal Auditors need to find our inspiration and resilience to overcome obstacles like those that Foghat faced, and be forward-looking, honest, candid, and impactful, as Lemmy most certainly was. Think of this book less as a traditional, cover-to-cover read and more as your own rock-and-roll setlist for Internal Audit.

Each chapter stands on its own, like a track on a classic album. You can drop the needle anywhere and still find the rhythm. Whether you're looking to fine-tune stakeholder relationships, elevate the impact of your reporting, harness data analytics and AI tools, strengthen your team culture, or navigate the complexities of audit committees, you'll find riffs and solos throughout that you can apply straight away.

The intent is not to lecture, but to guide. My goal is to give you practical, experience-driven ideas that you can remix for your own environment.

Like any great gig, the energy builds when you make it your own. So, use this book as your backstage pass and open it where it speaks loudest to your current challenge, and let the insights, stories, and lessons amplify your professional sound.

Internal Auditors and assurance professionals are a wonderful global community who care deeply about the organizations they work for. We want management to thrive. The Institute of Internal Auditors has done an excellent job promulgating internal auditing standards and supporting the development of internal auditing as a worthy profession globally.

This book references many great rock musicians. To celebrate their influence, I've created a companion Spotify playlist to accompany the book. Scan the QR code below to access the Internal Audit Rockstar playlist.

So, Internal Audit Rock Stars, are you ready to grab the mic and rock?

Shane M. Rogers, FCA MBA

Syosset, New York

March 17, 2026

Chapter 1

LIFE LESSONS LEARNT

Working as a Chartered Accountant in Dublin and New York

Accountants are often stereotyped these days. Rigid, by the numbers, tax gurus, conservative, and boring are all phrases and descriptions that come to mind. While a lot of it is, of course, in jest, there will always be some people who have a negative view of accountants. Luckily, the movie *The Accountant,*[9] starring Ben Affleck, has given us a new edgy persona. Accountants are cool these days, despite his character's penchant for rough justice.

I passed my final admitting examinations for Chartered Accountants Ireland back in 1991 and completed my 'articles' as an articled clerk to a Price Waterhouse Partner in 1993. Since then, I have been proud to call myself an accountant, or more precisely, an Irish Chartered Accountant. More specifically, I am proud to

---

9 *The Accountant*, released in 2016, written by Bill Dubuque, directed by Gavin O'Connor and starring Ben Affleck.

identify closely with the Internal Audit community, and I worked in Internal Audit roles for most of my career.

Accountants are real professionals, and the rigorous training and opportunities to grow and blaze your own trail in accounting and auditing firms around the globe are second to none. To me, Chartered Accountancy gives you a blank canvas, and it is up to you what colors you put on it. I chose Internal Audit because of the critical thinking, intrigue as to how businesses operate, and the satisfaction garnered from board reporting and impact.

Working for Price Waterhouse in the nineties was a great experience, though you were thrown into the deep end of the pool. It was sink or swim for sure. When you work for great people, you must immediately up your game to survive, pick up a lot of good habits, and learn by osmosis, just by being in the office and observing how executives respond to inquiries, pressure, how they engage clients, and sell assurance services. Public accounting firms are great places to work and learn, even if you often work late into the evening. The camaraderie is second to none.

When I was in Price Waterhouse Dublin, almost without fail, hordes of us would meet up for drinks in a few of the local pubs close to our offices on Friday evenings. No matter where the audit job was in Ireland, most audit teams made it back to Dublin for Friday drinks. There was a shared and very positive esprit de corps among the team of hundreds of Chartered Accountants. The partners would typically buy a couple of early rounds and then drift away as the younger crowd was left. Ahh, the good old times, and of course, it was great to be part of the younger crowd back then. We didn't have a lot of money, but we had lots of opportunities to learn, grow, and move up the ranks.

In Price Waterhouse New York, we had similar times, but drinks were more for a group or client group, given the office was so much larger. We worked hard, but we played hard too. Back in the early 1990s, the busy season hours in New York were insane; sometimes I felt like a walking zombie at work, I was so sleep-deprived, but I got used to it like everyone else in the same boat; we didn't have much choice in the matter, to be blunt. Working eighty or ninety hour weeks during the busy season was not uncommon.

I worked in the investment companies and funds group for a couple of years before moving to CS First Boston Internal Audit. The people in Price Waterhouse New York were a fantastic bunch. Standards were high, and our audit workpapers were tightly documented; everything was very precise, as the profession in the United States is more rules-driven than judgment-driven, as it was back home at that time.

In Ireland, back then, the partners exercised more professional judgment on achieving a 'true and fair' view in the financial statements. Since my early training years, global financial systems integration and consolidation of the larger public accounting firms have resulted in auditing practices becoming more standardized and rule-driven.

My favorite review note of all time was from one of my senior managers, Art. Reading his scrawl was tough, but it read "there is a 'rat' in separate," as he looked to correct my poor spelling. When it came to investment fund rules and accounting, Art was on the same level as Einstein. If you mentioned to a client that Art had a question, they would drop everything to understand what he was asking about and why. He was that good. Art was terrific.

Key Competencies I Learnt as a Chartered Accountant

At Price Waterhouse, I always recall how clear client communications were. While we performed financial statement audit work and rendered opinions on the financial statements and disclosures, I was always impressed with how new services were offered. A new rule or regulation might be coming out, and every decent company needs to have an independent review to assess readiness. Work proposals were always reasoned, budgeted costs were clear, and relevant experts participating were set forth.

There was always an element of proactive client communication and looking for opportunities to help them get ready for the next big change in business practice or regulations. We performed audits to high standards, but one-off special assignments were lucrative and typically more exciting to be involved in as a young accountant.

Our work always had a beginning, a middle, and an end. We performed audits typically in two phases: interim work before year-end to get ready, pick samples, and send out standard letters of request for receivables, bank loans, etc. Then we would come back post year-end to perform the substantial part of our audit and render an opinion on the financial statements. Deadlines were met to come hell or high water; everyone knew it, and we had to work late to ensure it happened. Clients really felt that their auditing firms cared about them.

As one very senior partner in Price Waterhouse Dublin explained to me when I was the junior accountant working on one of his client audits, "Clients pay for the name at the bottom of the audit opinion, son, they are paying for our high business and ethical standards, integrity and trust."

Integrity

When I left high school, I interned at a small Chartered Accounting firm in Dublin, Tynan and Dillon. I worked there for a few months during the Summer of 1987.

It was an interesting experience working in a small office located in an old Georgian-style house in Dublin city center. The team was great and knew their niche work, producing financial statements and tax returns for owner-managed businesses. My assigned job was to work on the accounts of one DJ Bannon, Esq, deceased. He ran a local store, and I worked on producing financial statements for the years 1985 and 1986.

I recall at the end of my internship, meeting with the lead partner, Barry Dillon. Barry liked my work and work ethic and was willing to offer me a place as an articled clerk with the firm (articled clerks were apprentices who learned the role of a Chartered Accountant under the tutelage of a qualified Chartered Accountant, typically a partner in a firm), while concurrently sitting a series of professional exams every year until qualified. Historically, it was how many Chartered Accountants started their careers right out of high school, but it was largely phased out a decade or two ago, as the profession required new students to have a university degree.

I shared that I had a couple of other offers, including one from Price Waterhouse. We chatted some more, but I remember his advice to me in the end: "Shane, if I had an offer from Price Waterhouse, I would choose it too!" As a partner and a person, he had integrity; he chose to steer me to a bigger firm with perhaps more to offer me than trying to convince me to stay with his firm. That resonated with me all these years, and I am grateful for Barry's advice. Thank you, Barry Dillon.

Respect for People and Words of Wisdom

One audit client I was assigned to back in Ireland was the Investment Bank of Ireland. It was a very convenient assignment for us because it was only 100 yards from our offices. The staff was professional and accommodating, and they had a decent cafeteria that you could use for free when assigned to their audits. I spent quite a lot of time there auditing mutual funds or UCITs (Undertakings for Collective Investment in Transferable Securities), as they are referred to in Europe.

The staff entrance was at the side of the building, at basement level, and the door was manned by Peter the Security Guard. Now, Peter was your typical tough Dubliner. There was no BS as he took his role seriously. His office had various certifications on the wall, and nobody was going through that door without the right credentials and badge.

I remember one fellow auditor just walking past and not showing his badge to Peter. He was immediately rebuked and ordered to come back and present himself. The person in question was not too happy about it and probably mumbled a few expletives under his breath, just out of Peter's earshot. I patiently waited for the storm in the teacup to be resolved. I presented my badge and greeted Peter as I always did. Peter looked at me and looked at the person ahead of me, who was making his way into the building by this stage.

"*Young man,*" he said, "*always treat people right on your way up the ladder. You never know when it will be your turn to come down the ladder, and you will need friends.*" Never were truer words said.

That was in the early 1990s. I suspect Peter has long since passed away, but his message still resonates. Have respect and treat others fairly. And I always have, so thank you, Peter, for your lifetime inspiration. Peter's words, simple as they may seem, have held me in good stead. At this juncture in my career, writing a book is a pivotal reflection point, looking back to look forward.

As a high schooler trying to assess what path to take, I remember having a chat with a longtime friend of my dad's, George Tracey. George was a very well-respected Chartered Accountant and Chief Financial Officer at a large, well-known financial institution in Ireland back in the eighties. I was torn between pursuing a career as an actuary or as a Chartered Accountant.

George's advice was simple: "*Shane, as a Chartered Accountant, you can do anything. You will be a mile wide and a few feet deep in terms of capabilities. If you choose the actuarial path, you will be a mile deep but only a few feet wide in terms of capabilities, as it is a more specialized profession. If you want to lead people, and if you want career optionality, the choice is obvious: become a Chartered Accountant.*" That was wonderful advice from a great person who has long since passed on. Thank you, George.

His advice, given to me as a high schooler in the late eighties, was so on the money. Actuaries are smart, capable people, but their roles are very specialized and technical. It is a great profession for those who excel at technical prowess, and even more so for those who can also explain and deliver such complex subject matter to the masses.

Triangulating Data Points and Opinions and Being Curious and Professionally Skeptical

When you work in a public auditing firm like I did, you learn to take everything you hear with a pinch of salt. While the story you may be hearing may be directionally correct, it may have a bit of spin on it. Some people, even clients, can be a bit economical with the truth at times. Some accounting treatment might be more favorable to them, and the auditors may catch it, or perhaps not.

We often played this game of silent chess when out in the field. We learned to trust our instincts and what we could support and validate. Our partners always asked great questions and had laser-beam focus on financial statement line items and differences period-to-period. They understood the economy, the company's margins and financing, its clients, and growth strategies, and they could sense very well if the overall big picture aligned with the various financial statement components.

As an audit junior or senior, you had to make sure your explanations made sense in the bigger picture. How could we support our assertions? How could we triangulate our explanations with fact patterns?

I remember one audit when I was an up-and-coming junior, where part of my role was to validate bank and loan balances. I had been on the interim audit and had the client's CFO sign a bunch of blank bank form letters for us to send out closer to year-end. Back in the office, I filled in all the banks I saw some historical activity on in the ledger. Come the year-end audit, one bank letter came back with a decent-sized loan at year-end, but when I reviewed the ledger the loan balance from that bank was zero.

Hmmm, I thought, that's a bit weird. Had the loan been repaid just prior to year-end, or had the bank made a mistake? So, I called the bank, and they were adamant that the loan was still outstanding, and the bank officer named the CFO as his key contact. The bank was not wrong, so where did the loan go?

I expanded all the entries for the loan account in the ledger and noticed the loan account was debited and a receivable account from their largest customer was credited with the amount of the loan. Cash was also transferred, crediting cash at the bank and debiting the receivable account. Very mysterious indeed. I asked myself, what is going on here?

Our client had decided to provide their largest customer with liquidity via a pass-through loan. The only problem was that the company was not authorized to make loans to customers, and the receivable balances, in hindsight, were likely not fully recoverable. It was unethical, ultra vires[10] the company's articles and memorandum of association, and a material window-dressing event or financial statement fraud.

Of course, we escalated it to our Manager and our Partner, who both agreed this was a big problem. We had to check and double-check our facts. Nobody wanted to accuse anyone of wrongdoing, but equally, if it walks like a duck and talks like a duck, it's a duck. For me, it was important to see how our Manager and Partner responded.

They asked all the right questions, and luckily for me, I had supporting documentation for all their questions. They kept coming back to the motive and why these entries might have been made. Why was the company providing liquidity and a loan to its largest customer? For context, during the late 1980s and early 1990s the Irish economy was limping along, trying to break out of a tough decade, the eighties, mired with political uncertainty, high unemployment, and poor economic growth.

They confronted the CFO and the CEO, and it all came out. Their largest client was in financial difficulty and could not get liquidity from the banks directly, so this company, a key supplier, decided to keep them afloat and provided some emergency financing. The client was told to reverse it all and correctly reflect the uncertainties in the financial statements, or we would have to resign as statutory auditors.

That was a very big step to threaten, but in effect, it put the audit firm's and partners' reputations above that of the client. It was a subsidiary of a large global group. Not bad for a wet-around-the-ears junior auditor like me! But even today, this example sticks with me. I recall a real sense of pride as the audit team

---

10 'Ultra Vires' is a Latin phrase meaning beyond the powers. In legal terms it means any action by a company or its agents that exceeds the legal scope of its authority.

had lunch later that week with our Partner and Manager, reflecting on the incident.

We had solved the riddle, acted ethically and with integrity, and I had played a leading role in discovering the concealed financial entries. When something does not seem right, you must lean in, learning more by asking questions. Being ethical is an absolute requirement to call yourself a Chartered Accountant or Internal Auditor. Ethics matter, and I had passed the test. Be curious, understand motives, and ask good questions; it pays dividends as an external or internal auditor.

Reading Between the Lines

This is a great skill to have in your arsenal, as it allows you to reconcile theory with the practicalities of life and work.

When I was training to be a Chartered Accountant back in the early nineties, I was asked to perform an inventory count at short notice one Friday afternoon. It suited me, as the stock count, as we called them, was at a wholesale paint distributor in the Bally Mount industrial estate, which was not too far from where I lived at the time, a Dublin suburb called Templeogue.

I arrived about three o'clock and knew I was probably working against the clock, given it was Friday afternoon. When I arrived, the manager and staff were waiting for me. A nice guy called John (Johner, as he was referred to) accompanied me and showed me the inventory. I stood out a bit, dressed in my pinstripe suit, briefcase in hand. It was their year-end, and if memory served me correctly, it was the end of June.

All was fine as we went into the warehouse, and I selected various higher-end paint products to count and check the tallies that management had made available. I took copies of the last five purchase orders received and the last five sales orders so we could perform some cut-off testing for the purchases and sales in their ledgers, which were all normal procedures. I was making good progress; lots of samples and good coverage would provide strong input into the year-end audit in the coming months.

As I selected one more item to count about five o'clock, there was a broadcast announcement across the warehouse PA system, delivered in a typical Dublin accent, flat and sarcastic:

"Paging Johner, paging Johner. The Cuckoo's Nest (the local pub) has been on, and they want to know if they should pull you one pint of Guinness, or two!"

Reading between the lines, I looked at Johner and said, *"This stock count is over!"*

"Ahh," he said, *"I'm glad you can take a hint."* We had a good laugh about it, as he noted they had had a rough week and a few pints for medicinal purposes were calling. The Cuckoo's Nest pub was on the way home, so I managed to hitch a lift in Johner's Nissan HiAce van at least to the Walkinstown roundabout and walked the last mile home from there.

Empathy

It was late summer at the tail end of the nineties, and this day was among the worst days of my Internal Audit career on Wall Street, not because of anything I did as an Audit Manager, but because of some questionable behavior by one of our bosses at Group Headquarters. Now, I am going to be a little vague on purpose, but I was on assignment in Brazil at the time, unrelated to the audit assignment I was also wrapping up in New York.

We had drafted a report, and it had many issues in it. Important issues, not because the management team was bad, but because their business was very specialized and very unorthodox relative to the other securities and loan businesses we operated. The draft report was shared with the Group Head of Internal Audit for review and comments, as was our standard process back then.

Unluckily, one of our Group Board Members just happened to stop by the Group Audit function on this day. By chance, the draft report, which had not yet been shared with the auditee management, was shown prematurely to this Board Member. Let's just say he blew a gasket when he read the draft issues in the report. He called the senior executive responsible for the US and read him the riot act. Shit flows downhill as we all know, and I was it.

All I could do was call the management team in question and apologize, sharing my empathy with them for the way they were treated and the unexpected Executive Management reaction to the draft report, particularly given that it had not yet completed our normal clearance process. What had transpired was simply not the way we operated and not the way I operated.

Upon my return to the office, we had a candid discussion about the issues, which we had already signaled to them throughout our fieldwork. I was clear that it was more the nature of their business, not fitting into our broader systems architecture, that was the root cause of many points. They understood that, and we met up the following week when I was back from Brazil. Yes, it was a bad report, but the context was made clear.

Every cloud has a silver lining, though. Happy to say, a year or so after our Internal Audit report was issued, the business in question was spun out. The management team, who were already Wall Street superstars, went on to become legends in their field of financial expertise. They were superstars to begin with, but in some strange sense, I hope my candid audit report helped them in becoming an independent business, which was a much better set-up for their very specialized operations.

Having Fun!

It is so important to have a sense of humor in performing our work. After all, auditing and internal auditing are work centered on finding problems, errors, or inconsistencies, and fixing them to help the business thrive. There is a lot to be said about having fun, and certainly in my years in public accounting in Ireland, we had tons of it! Many of the shenanigans cannot be shared here, as you can probably appreciate; the nineties were a very different time and place.

Glass Cutters or Glass Blowers – You Decide?

I do recall, though, one poor junior auditor who was convinced by his managers to manually count glass cutters and blowers as they entered a glass factory one day because they suspected payroll fraud. To be honest, this junior accountant had a reputation for being a bit on the cocky side; my sense is this joke was intended to bring him down a notch or two to reality, Irish style! Of course, it was all a ruse, and it was one of those Irish days when it rained non-stop.

This poor chap stood out in the lashing rain all day under a large golf umbrella, clipboard in hand, and tried to tally the two types of staff. His only guidance on how to differentiate the two types of employees was to look at people's lips; the glassblowers have bigger lips, given the work they do! How they convinced him to do this with straight faces must have been acting worthy of an Academy Award, red-carpet material.

At the team dinner that night, he came in, soaked to the bone, and reported his numbers, which were something like 552 cutters and 367 glassblowers. His reporting rendered the rest of the audit team almost unconscious with laughter, never mind the copious amounts of drink being consumed. This prank was one for the record books.

So, whenever you think you are having a bad day, think about this poor sod and what he had to endure as a rite of passage in the auditing world! After that, your day will be rocking for sure.

The Manager Impersonator Strikes Again!

In another firm, there was the Leonard case. A great friend of mine, Del, explained to me that Leonard was a Senior Manager with a very distinct accent. One of the audit seniors was great at impersonating him. Every now and again, some unsuspecting junior, who was waiting to be assigned work at his desk, would receive a phone call: "*This is Leonard, can you get the files for client X from the file room and bring them to my office?*"

Back in the late eighties and early nineties, we all still had physical audit files and workpapers, as the transition to electronic media was in the very early stages.

Sure enough, fifteen minutes later, a young lad would knock on Leonard's door and drop all the file boxes in. Leonard would, of course, respond, "*What are you doing? I didn't ask for these files.*" The unsuspecting junior auditor would bring the files back to the central filing room and return to his desk.

A few minutes later, he would be called again by the impersonator: "*This is Leonard, can you bring me the files for client X to my office? What is taking you so long? I have an accountancy practice to run here. Hurry up.*" The junior would again attempt to deliver the files and again get rebuked by Leonard in his strange accent: "*Are you mad? Get these files out of here. I told you before that I did not request these files. Is there something wrong with you?*"

The poor junior would get back to his desk, only this time he received a round of applause from his colleagues, who were all in on the joke. The impersonator made himself public, and the whole team reflected on the recent goings-on. Even Leonard opened his office door to see what all the fuss and noise was about. That junior was neither the first nor the last to fall for this prank. Poor bastard!

Registered Audit Tick Marks, Anybody?

Yes, every year, there were all sorts of fun being had, largely at the junior auditors' expense. It was an unwritten rite of passage. Every year, several teams of juniors would make the pilgrimage to the Institute of Chartered Accountants (now known as Chartered Accountants Ireland) headquarters to register their audit tick marks,[11] having been instructed to do so by their audit seniors and managers. It was all in jest, of course, and the institute staff were very polite in redirecting the hordes of young, fresh-faced junior accountants back to their offices, with their tails between their legs, but the new intake didn't always know.

Unassigned Staff Member Collects a Dubious Prescription

Among the best pranks played during my time working in Dublin was when a junior accountant was asked to go collect a prescription, or so he thought, for one of our partners. That morning, a prankster audit senior had crafted a 'medical prescription' in a small envelope and left it with the Partner's Secretary.

The prankster, impersonating the partner, summoned one of the unassigned staff to come up and fill his prescription at the

11 Audit tick marks are symbols or notations used by auditors during the audit process to document their work and to denote auditing actions taken during testing or review activities.

pharmacy across the road from the office. A ten-pound note was left with the envelope on the Secretary's desk. It all sounded legit, and it checked out. So, this junior accountant, who had nothing better to do at the time, took the envelope and cash and sauntered off to the local pharmacy. Not thinking much about it, he handed the envelope to the pharmacist and waited, as you do, for a prescription to be filled.

A few minutes later, there was a lot of laughter among the pharmacy staff. The junior was a bit perplexed. He was just running an errand, presumably for antibiotics or some other required medication. What was going on? They gave him back his envelope and a paper bag with a box of condoms. The pharmacist suggested he look at the prescription.

The 'prescription' was in fact a handwritten note along these lines: Hi, my name is Brendan (not his real name) and I'm very shy, and I need to buy some condoms. Please put them quietly in a brown paper bag, and I will furnish you with a ten-pound note. Love is in the air tonight!'

The junior was mortified, of course, and when he got back to the office, the entire team on his floor awaited his return. Yes, it was embarrassing, but sidesplittingly funny nonetheless!

We had fun times and real camaraderie. You had to have your wits about you, though, as there was always the risk of being had. Fun at your expense lurked around every corner of the office, and this constant screening of requests and being cautious probably helped many of us sharpen our skills in picking up on things that were not quite right or did not compute, the unwritten part of our training.

Having fun was a great pressure-release valve. While some of these anecdotes might not fly in today's office culture, generally, within a team, having fun and not taking yourselves too seriously are great ways to build esprit de corps.

Recap of Key Learnings in this Chapter:

1. Inspiration and words of wisdom are to be found in many aspects of everyday interactions and life. Tune into these opportunities and heed life lessons from your network of friends, family, and work colleagues. Who is your George Tracey or Peter the Security Guard, and what simple life rules can you take from their example?

2. Successful Internal Auditors can benefit from my simple code: always conduct yourself with integrity, be respectful, demonstrate good ethical behaviors, be curious, demonstrate empathy, and of course, have fun.

3. Don't take yourself too seriously. Ignore the human element at your peril.

Chapter 2

HISTORICAL TRUTHS

AND MISCONCEPTIONS THAT HAUNT INTERNAL AUDIT

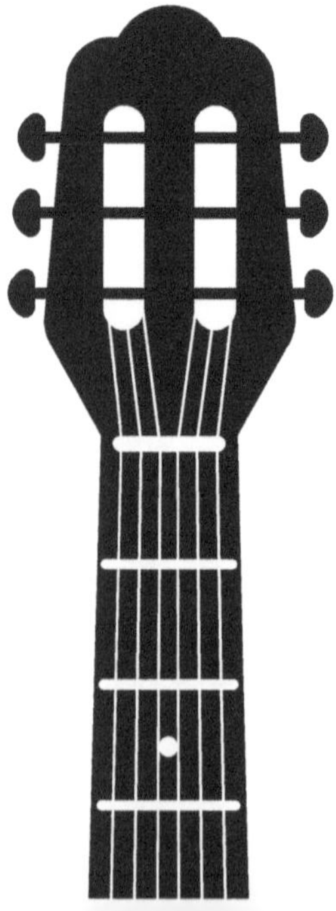

Having spent almost twenty years of my career in Internal Audit, I have picked up on many aspects of internal auditing that, at times can really let the side down.

Don't get me wrong, many of these truths have been focused on, and good progress has been made by many audit departments in recent years, thankfully. However, there is no doubt in my mind that there are plenty of Internal Audit teams out there who need to review this list closely. Below, I discuss six truths, or elephants in the room, that Internal Audit leaders should reflect on.

1 – Internal Audit Is Failing to Connect with Management

Why do so many internal auditors struggle to make meaningful relationship connections with management?

Investing in relationships with management and selling risk coverage, business or technology performance assessment and assurance are Internal Audit 101 activities. Notwithstanding this, few Internal Auditors that I know have invested in sales skills, and thus it is no surprise that many in management would describe a meeting with Internal Audit as only slightly better than going to the dentist for an emergency root canal.

Midway in my career in Investment Banking, I spent four years supporting the Fixed Income Strategic Client Coverage team. They were experienced sales executives who sold the bank's overall fixed income product set and debt capital markets capabilities to institutional clients. They were in the business of relationship sales, rather than being transactional counterparties.

They sold the big picture, the possibilities, and the dream. They cared about their clients in a big picture sense and how each product salesperson serviced their needs, asked for feedback, and looked to add value in any way they could. The overall health of the big picture mattered as much as each of the individual product sale components. That built client trust, and some of these relationships grew exponentially over the four years I had the privilege of being a supporting part of that great team. Fast-forward a few years to the global financial crisis, and I took this relationship sales approach to Internal Audit and never looked back.

Internal Auditors love formality, structure, and details, and we never fail to write everything down. I mean everything. I recall many times management executives raising eyebrows as they witnessed the documentation of their meeting with Internal Audit. Scary stuff indeed, and nothing is more off-putting than the feeling that every word you utter is being written down. Court stenographers struggle to take as many copious notes as some of our Internal Audit colleagues. Ideally, we should be more in listening mode and only jot down key learnings or actions in these meetings. Luckily, we have AI tools these days to help us, so there are no more excuses.

There is no need to take minutes of relationship meetings in a he-said or she-said style, as this is wasteful and may indicate that we are not listening properly or capturing the right context. A few bullet points of learnings and action steps would suffice, and these days, we can leverage AI tools to readily summarize meetings and outline key learnings and actions. Also, relationship meetings should always be driven by a one or two-page agenda. Again, just a few key headings to touch upon.

Keeping things informal really helps, as management will feel more at ease and not under the spotlight. Importantly, Internal Audit and any Coordinated Assurance Partners in attendance (it is a great practice to meet management stakeholders together using a shared agenda) should also have a couple of topics to give back to management. These can be updates on new rules or regulations (Compliance), operational events and near misses (Risk Management), relevant firmwide insights or updates on Audit's vision, rotation or job swap opportunities in Audit, etc.

Quarterly relationship meetings are useful and can really help Internal Auditors build trust with management as you look for ways to demonstrate value outside of the formal transactional audit cycle. Much more on this topic in Chapter 14.

Some internal auditors walk on eggshells and are afraid to help the business here and now, for example, by giving feedback on a draft policy document or a business plan. While we all take pride in being objective and independent, if management is asking you for your input, provide it. They value what you have to say. Couch your feedback any way you want but provide it and be helpful. It is the least you can do to help the business out and with such gestures, you will build trust.

2 – Internal Audit Can Come Across as the Unrealistic World of Perfection

Being a perfectionist is simply not part of an internal auditor's job description.

Some roles in society require extremely technical skills and a perfectionist bent to be successful.

For example, a pilot, a nuclear engineer running a power station, or an astrophysicist measuring the path of an asteroid hurtling toward Earth. People in these types of roles must be exceptionally well-trained, as perfection is the expected outcome all the time.

Being an Internal Auditor is not one of those roles, but many Internal Auditors come across as perfectionists. What do I mean? Failing to grasp the big picture, clinging to low-level details that do not really matter, ticking and tying in the last few weeks of an audit to produce the perfect file, with no real impact in terms of issues or insights for management consumption. Let me be clear, while Internal Auditors need to be thorough and commercial, perfectionism has a high cost.

Luckily, in recent years, the emergence and adoption of agile auditing in many audit teams has exposed perfectionist audit practices. To be commercial and responsive to risk, Internal Auditors need to assess risks more broadly and use their judgement when concluding their work. We must be reasoned and objective and have clear supporting evidence for our observations and conclusions; we need to be good or great, but not perfect. This is a broader risk culture topic for Internal Audit teams to debate, to ensure that a very conservative, perfectionist style is replaced by a more engaging, agile, and risk-responsive style.

Many Internal Auditors that I know have a perfectionist streak in them. Sometimes we jokingly referred to this as *auditors' disease*, or not knowing when to stop. If we are not up to our necks in detail, then we may be pondering why the business has not documented everything perfectly.

One must stop and remind oneself of what the Internal Audit team is there to do when you boil everything down. No matter the formal words of our audit charters and methodologies, our core reason to be is to make the business enterprise better, better risk understanding, better controls design and operation, better results, and better outcomes.

I recall at the start of my career in public accounting seeing a cartoon taped to an office window in a client's office where we were performing the year-end external audit. It read: "Watch out, '*the Odditors*' are here".

Beside it was another cartoon of a fallen medieval soldier on the battlefield being finished off by a modern office worker (Auditor) wielding a large sword with a caption, '*Beware the Auditors are Bayoneting the Wounded after the Battle.*' Quite amusing to me at the time, to be honest, as the audit junior on the job, but the more I reflect on the cartoon decades later, the more I can relate to the subliminal messaging hidden therein.

As auditors, we can come across as a bit odd given our penchant for formality, signoffs, documentation, and perfection at times, at least that is how many in management perceive us. Many of us are likely guilty of seeing the world of risks and controls through our own blinkered vision rather than through the eyes of business management. We should always be objective and inquisitive, but the more we put ourselves in management's shoes, the better our engagement and solutions focus will be. We will be more empathetic and reasonable.

When I worked with the relationship managers within Fixed Income Sales, you could understand their need for speed, but it was always progress over perfection; they were very smart and laser-focused on achieving great outcomes for their clients.

Conversations mattered. Intent mattered. Speed and response time mattered. Outcomes mattered. Documentation and controls did not matter to quite the same intense extent, as they operated largely based on trust.

Do not misunderstand me, controls still mattered, but you could understand how such outcomes-focused salespeople could be consumed by client wins, wallet share growth, and new deals rather than documentation evidencing internal controls. Of course, the Fixed Income sales team had a Chief Operating Officer who knew when to focus on their key controls and ensure key decisions and outcomes were being evidenced.

The Fixed Income team also knew how to have fun. One of our colleagues was a great guy called Kirk. He had a gentle soul, about 5'8 and weighing about 110 pounds on a wet day. One day, one of our Information Technology team members was on the phone with him and needed to come down to look at Kirk's computer. The IT person asked how he would identify Kirk in the sea of trading desks, as we had row after row of them and worked on one of the biggest trading floors in the world back in the day.

"Don't worry," Kirk said, "you can't miss me, I'm about 6' 10" and 300 pounds, about the same size as Hulk Hogan." Soon afterward, we all noticed this perplexed IT guy reviewing each trading desk, up and down, up and down, clearly looking for a veritable giant. The laughs we had when the not-so-giant Kirk revealed himself.

Do our stakeholders and management value our work, impact, communication, and other outputs to the extent we perceive them to be valuable?

That may be a bit of an aha moment for some Internal Auditors. Returning to the cartoon story, the second cartoon has perhaps a more subtle message about value. As Internal Auditors, we all feel we add great value to our clients and organizations, but we should periodically reflect on our sources of value for the business and our relevance.

The auditor in the cartoon was being merciless, presumably finishing off a soldier who was already dying. You can understand the implied question of relevance and value. Internal Auditors need not compromise being objective and independent, but we should try to understand the real pressure of business and management life better.

Ask your stakeholders openly for feedback on Internal Audit's relevance, value for money, risk agility, and overall usefulness. You might be surprised by what they tell you. Either way, you may come away with valuable insights to help you and your team be more effective. In and around your off-cycle relationship meetings with management, periodically ask for some feedback and look to act on it visibly. Stakeholders will appreciate Internal Audit listening and taking feedback on, and while it works both ways, these types of interactions build trust.

3 – Internal Audit May Be Selling a Product That Management Doesn't Really Value

Is Internal Audit selling a product that nobody wants to buy?

Selling is a core Internal Audit activity in my view, but unfortunately, it is not an area that many Internal Auditors have historically focused on. As I sit here in 2025 penning this book, it feels imperative that Internal Audit teams take a good, hard look in the mirror and self-assess their sources of differentiated value. Let me be blunt: other than for small audit teams, sample-based audits should be consigned to history.

Modern systems and scalable data analysis should drive full-data audits using hypotheses to determine overall data conformance. Agile auditing should drive greater risk responsiveness, and audit plans should be quarterly rather than annual.

When external or internal events crop up suddenly, for example, the collapse of Silicon Valley Bank and Signature Bank in March 2023, Internal Auditors need to react. Agile Internal Audit teams would have updated their Audit Committees in April with new audits in areas like Treasury, Capital Management, and Risk Scenario Management.

Think about it. If the Head of Internal Audit came back and told the Audit Committee about these risk areas, only to add that they would consider them for next year's audit plan, that person would be laughed out of the room! There is great value in being responsive to risk, and Internal Auditors should be having risk responsive conversations with their Audit Committee Chair.

Being sample-based, backward-looking, and operating on an annual cycle is eighties thinking. Some Chief Audit Executives believe it is better to keep the status quo and avoid too much change. If you have an annual audit plan, perform sample-based audits, and are not auditing key risks here and now, I have news for you: you run the risk of being part of the problem when a large operational or financial risk materializes. Nobody is saying change is easy. It takes courage and sustained effort to shape a new norm within an Internal Audit function, especially for smaller teams. Having the courage to speak up can be a catalyst for changing minds.

The good news is that even a one-person team can adopt core agile principles and deliver more valuable work. More about this topic a bit later.

4 – Failing to Deliver Value-for-Money Audits

Should value delivery, impact and quality feedback be our yardsticks rather than audit scope coverage?

As a Chief Audit Executive, I often asked my team members two simple questions about each audit: What does good look like? What does great look like?

Of course, these simple questions often had complex answers, given the scope of our audit, business complexities, and systems. We were an agile audit team, and we took pride in wrapping up audits at the right time to avoid wasting our scarce audit resources on low-risk areas. This was especially true if the first few sprints had gone well and had few observations or exceptions (more on sprints and agile auditing in Chapter 6).

Almost all our audits were data-driven, using hypotheses to test full data populations, and our approach was to prioritize the most important areas first. It was fine in our world to issue a positive A- or B-rated audit report if we reached that conclusion quickly, and we normally completed these audits, start to finish, in eight to ten weeks.

There is a big opportunity cost to over-auditing low-level risks, as Internal Audit may fail to cover key risk areas in its audit pipeline. Audit Committees, Audit Chairs, and Executive Management want current and relevant audit reports, and it is critical that internal audits really question the timeframe to perform and issue audits and assess product agility.

There are many ways for Internal Audit to provide assurance on key risks and controls, and we will touch upon some options in a later chapter. Suffice it to say, if your team takes five months to issue audit reports with few or no issues, you are neither concluding nor failing fast enough.

The silver lining is that your team has great opportunities to improve risk responsiveness and product agility. No matter the audit team size, everyone can adopt agile principles such as using two-week sprints, sprint reviews, and team retrospectives to continually improve, refine, and redirect work. Agile is a value-driven mindset.

5 – Our Tendency to Issue Verbose, Poorly Worded Audit Reports

Every audit report has a unique tone, just like every rock band has its sound.

I could probably write an entire book on this topic alone. Note to self. During my time in banking and reinsurance companies, we devoted quite a bit of training time to communication skills and, specifically, audit issue and report writing. It's a real shame when we perform great audits, only to fall at the last hurdle by issuing reports full of jargon and audit-speak. If we are not careful, we could cause widespread confusion, even panic, among our stakeholders and Executive Management if the words we choose are not fit for purpose.

Another important consideration is the overall tone of the audit report. Just as in a rock band, it is the tone that ultimately differentiates the band's sound. Some bands just have it, and their music, no matter the song, is instantly recognizable. For example, Queen, The Rolling Stones, Van Halen, and Motörhead all fall into that category for me, as they are instantly identifiable and unique. Likewise, in Internal Audit parlance, it is important to keep the tone balanced with the severity of the issues being reported. Another key consideration for Internal Auditors is to resist the temptation to overstate actual or perceived risks.

There is no magic formula to determine whether an audit report overall is satisfactory or unsatisfactory, but in my experience, all too often, Internal Auditors are very conservative, and some tend to overstate risks. Auditor judgment is critical, and the issues raised must be assessed relative to the depth and breadth of the audit scope.

I recall that when working in banking, many of our audits were global in nature, and when we combined issues from four regional teams together, the reports often had many issues and were typically rated as unsatisfactory. Indeed, it was quite rare to issue a global audit report that was not unsatisfactory, and with the benefit of many years' hindsight, that no longer feels right to me.

When working in insurance, our audit report conclusions included clear statements on whether we agreed, partially agreed, or disagreed with management's self-assessment. An unsatisfactory audit report driven by management self-identified issues would be considered a relatively good outcome, as the Audit Committee would note that management was aware of the key issues and had self-raised corrective actions in advance of the Internal Audit. Fair point. We would agree with their self-assessment, and the Audit Committee and Board felt comfortable that management was on top of its game and had adequate remediation plans in progress.

As a sparring partner, I always provided feedback on draft management self-assessments before accepting them as final. For example, did the narrative match the objectives and self-ratings? For me, this step was important to help management reflect upon the task at hand.

Some peers called me soft, or perhaps too nice, but my feedback on their draft assessments was exactly the opposite. It was direct, openly questioning their wording, logic, and at times their self-ratings, not to help me or the audit, but to help management to be honest and candid in describing their key risks and internal controls. As management self-assessments were part of our audit report, these few pages would be read by the Chairman and the Board. So, it is better to be open, honest, and candid upfront, rather than winging it and hoping for the best. This practice helped me demonstrate to management that I cared about their business and their reputations, effectively building trust.

6 – Internal Audit Is Often Perceived by Management as the Enemy. Is Our Feedback Not Valued by Management?

Why are so many Internal Audit teams still considered by management to be cops rather than trusted business partners?

In many organizations, there is often a belief among management that we are out to get them. Is it a deep-rooted fear of being embarrassed or put on the defensive by surprise audit issues? Or is it because management fears the reaction of the Board and Audit Committee if the audit report highlights big issues that they did not self-identify? Does management think we want them to be fired?

To try and answer these questions we must review how Internal Audit is positioned, how our services are valued and how the organization embraces the gift of feedback from audit reports. Sadly, some Chief Audit Executives relish politics and twist audit outcomes to rain misery down on management. Thankfully, such people do not normally last too long in an organization and typically find themselves victims of their own medicine.

One CEO I recall was very vehement about feedback being a gift to embrace and to be thankful for. His message resonated with his board members, and it was not unusual for the board member responsible for the area being audited to thank the audit team in writing for their work and observations. They typically did this by responding to everyone copied on the email when the audit report and insights memo were distributed.

That messaging was well received, and it struck a good risk culture note and set an excellent tone at the top and the board members thanked the Internal Audit team irrespective of whether the report was satisfactory or unsatisfactory.

I also recall another CEO who attended an Audit Committee Meeting where we presented an unsatisfactory audit report with several significant issues. He accepted the audit report and added very complimentarily that it took a tough internal audit report to help management reflect on the business risks and challenges they were facing at the time. As a result, they had identified several additional actions they planned to take on top of the audit points. Internal audit was a real catalyst, spurring the business on to achieve greater things.

Too often, management's pushback is driven by their fears and sensitivities to executive reaction to our audit issues and ratings. It is critical that the Audit Committee and CEO set the right tone from the top. When there is an unsatisfactory audit report, management should help deliver the messages to the Audit Committee and Board, their accountability, their learnings, and their plans to remediate. Let's not forget our role, when you boil it all down, it is to help the business be successful. Identifying gaps and weaknesses in risk understanding and controls so they can be fixed.

Personally, I am a fan of rating issues to help prioritize remedial actions. Audit issues are specific weaknesses that can be sized and can be addressed. Overall audit report ratings are useful in corporate governance and stewardship capacities as they can provide a great relative comparison or look across the organization. Rating audit reports is an area where we must be both careful and diligent so that we do not overstate the risks. Let's be honest, the sky should not be falling on every other audit.

Management competence may be unfairly questioned at times, and our report ratings may be used by some political people to damage careers and promote stereotyping. Of course, management must be accountable, and there will be times when perhaps the only conclusion the Audit Committee and Board can fairly reach is that a particular management team is simply not good enough.

In my career, I have issued hundreds of audit reports and edited and reviewed thousands more, and a fair share of them (I would guess 20 – 25%) were unsatisfactory outcomes. With digital scorecards and reports available on demand these days, audit reports perhaps are not really required as we slice and dice all the audit issues quite easily. Being progressive requires Internal Audit to find new solutions to old problems.

It is not a blame game, and Boards and Audit Committees should accept Internal Audit reports and issues as the ultimate corporate feedback. When management is open and has lots of informal dialogue with Internal Audit every quarter, the organization's risk and control culture will prosper. Internal Auditors need to invest more time in relationships with management, particularly the informal cycle of meetings and insight sharing. This takes effort, as many Internal Auditors and accountants love structure and formality. Being informal builds trust and shows that we care (we revisit this topic in more detail in Chapter 14). We want the business and organization to be successful beyond its wildest dreams. We want to help businesses expand, grow, and scale with confidence. We want to identify weaknesses early so they can be corrected. We are partners with management, and we should market these efforts more effectively. Yes, we are independent and objective, but let's not hide behind that veil so much. Being transparent is among the best approaches that can help Internal Audit's reputation with management. Our audit work is the ultimate business feedback, a gift that is well-intended, objective, and supported with facts.

Motörhead's Superfans: The Measure of an Indispensable Feedback Loop!

Recent decades have witnessed the advent of 'superfans,' fans of music artists who often take extended vacations to follow their favorite artist or band on tour. As fans, they are the epitome of a feedback loop, they are heavily invested in the band's tour schedule, loyal, critical and candid. They want to see a great show, night after night. Motörhead was one of these bands with superfans.

In their 2005 documentary *Live Fast Die Old,*[12] there is a backstage scene with a gathering of Motörhead superfans who were following the band on their 2003 UK tour of eleven cities. All were stereotypical biker types, clad in denim and leather, tattoos, etc. However, as we all know, looks can be deceiving.

Delving a little deeper, they clearly articulated their collective mission, their love of the band and its music and their passion for the band's music. They were loyal, reliable and well-spoken in all aspects of Motörhead. Lead singer and bass player, Lemmy, noted that "he relies on the superfans to let him know that they are doing things right", and he openly acknowledges their

12 *Motörhead: Live Fast Die Old* documentary, 2005, directed by Alex Berk, with Miranda Sawyer, Lemmy Kilmister, Phil Campbell and Mikkey Dee.

superfans as "great people", which is great recognition of the power and value of a good feedback loop to keep the band honest and true to its rock and roll roots and to its fanbase.

There is an interesting analogy to my earlier CEO and board member example. Lemmy, in effect, was the CEO of Motörhead (any professional band is a business undertaking, often a partnership), and he absolutely valued candid superfan feedback and openly praised them for it. Makes you think, right?

Motörhead treated these fans with great respect; gave them their own backstage dressing room and show passes, etc. and indeed the band members formed many long-lasting friendships with these superfans. That kind of mutual respect is exactly what we as internal auditors should aspire to in our relationship with management. We all should ask ourselves: do we have such a high-quality feedback loop from our stakeholders and auditees that Motörhead had?

Many of us could learn valuable lessons from Motörhead. Peel back the gruff exterior, and you might be amazed at the leadership qualities you find. Let's not forget, Lemmy Kilmister's lifelong desire was simply to be remembered as an honest man. May he rest in peace, not just as a great rock and roll musician and an honest man, but also as an inspiration to Internal Auditors the world over.

Recap of Key Learnings in this Chapter:

1. Invest in your relationships with management and demonstrate that as an Internal Auditor you care about their business, its success and performance. Sales and relationship management skills are critical to positioning Internal Audit as being much more than a transactional counterparty in the eyes of management.

2. It is not the role of Internal Auditors to be perfect, and perfectionism has a real cost associated with it, and most of us cannot afford it. My advice, good to great, is good enough.

3. Internal Auditors must be responsive to risks and agile to add value to their organizations. Even if your audit team is small to medium-sized, don't be afraid to adopt agile principles such as performing work in sprints, holding team retrospectives, and promoting continuous learning. Don't be afraid to demonstrate your risk responsiveness.

4. Focus on adding value to your organization and use agile methodologies or principles to allocate your scarce resources in covering your key risk domains. Leverage product agility to increase

Recap of Key Learnings in this Chapter:

the effectiveness of your risk coverage and reporting. Eliminate low-risk testing.

5. Incorporate management self-assessments into your audit reports to add transparency on the risk and control environment to the Audit Committee and Board. Help management to be open, honest, and candid in their self-assessment. Pre-audit, engage openly with management on their self-assessment, their logic, their demonstration of key risk and control awareness and their risk culture, transparency, and accountability. More on the topic of management self-assessments in chapter 7.

6. Look to your CEO and Audit Committee to help establish the right tone at the top; ask management to help present unsatisfactory audit reports and to demonstrate their accountability and ownership more directly to the Audit Committee and Board.

7. Consider your audit report the ultimate management feedback loop, just like Motörhead's superfans. Share and ask for open, honest, and candid feedback, just like Motörhead did.

Chapter 3

BOSSES GIVE ORDERS, While Internal Audit Leaders Choose to Coach

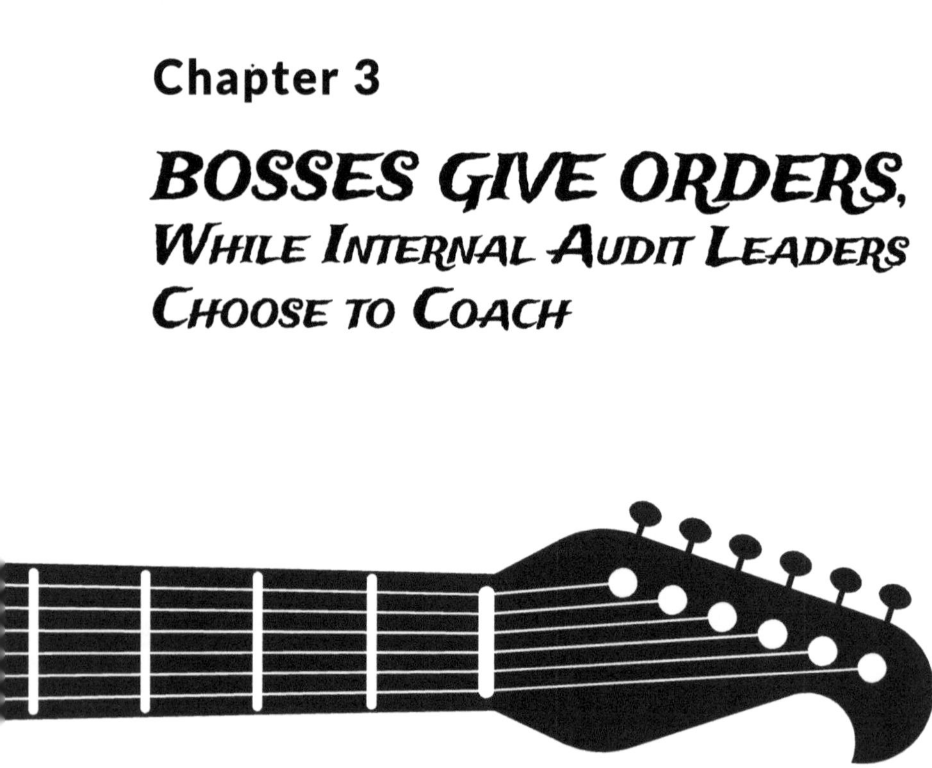

Coaching is a critical part of helping up-and-coming Internal Auditors excel and make the leap from 'effective doer and reporter' to 'inspiring leader.' We can all relate to working for a manager or boss at some point in our careers, who simply was not effective. We all can probably recall performing great work that resonated with peers and clients, only to be torn to shreds by the boss! A tough spot to be in, no doubt about it. As we mature, we can more readily recognize that some people are simply not leaders of teams and people. Bosses are rigid, self-centered, and often the epitome of what is wrong with corporate culture.

It is sad, really. Many of us can agree that working for a boss, in every sense of that word, can be among the most soul-destroying experiences of one's life. What irks me most is that many Human Resources departments and so-called people experts remain silent, allowing entire teams to suffer rather than standing up and demanding better leaders. Get the people equation right, and you are off to the races. Get it wrong, and you will struggle to add value to your organization.[13]

Leaders make great coaches, and being a coach within Internal Audit is a critically important undertaking. That said, it is not easy and takes an open mind and perseverance to show results. I always liked to coach team members to help them grow. In our team, the aspiration was that everyone could make it to the Chief Audit Executive level eventually. Of course, that may be quite difficult to achieve, but having the right aspiration is important.

Self-motivation, self-investment, and continuous learning help talented people develop and allow leaders to emerge. In visionary and continuous improvement terms, the journey taken is often more valuable than reaching the planned destination. An Internal Audit team comprised of leaders who are passionate about their roles and want to grow and add value together is far better than a team of individuals or aspiring bosses.

Leadership lessons don't just come from boardrooms or audit committees. Sometimes they emerge from the most unexpected places, like a swamp in Florida.

Was Lynyrd Skynyrd's Ronnie Van Zant an Agile Coach Back in the Early Seventies?

Most people have heard of Lynyrd Skynyrd, the seventies southern rock band that unfortunately suffered a plane crash at the height of its fame in 1977, killing several band members and injuring

13 Gallup, State of the Global Workplace 2023 Report (Washington, D.C.: Gallup Press, 2023), https://www.gallup.com/workplace/349484/state-of-the-global-workplace.aspx

the others.[14] For a rock band, they had some unique traits. One, they were among the most rehearsed bands ever.

In the 2018 movie about Lynyrd Skynyrd, *If I Leave Here Tomorrow*,[15] written and directed by Stephen Kijak, their producer recalled how he was in awe that at rehearsal before recording, every take sounded the same. Just great. As a producer, he had relatively little to do. This was a band of leaders. This was very unusual, but it showed that the band had perfected each song and worked in unison together.

With most bands, there is a certain level of ad-libbing with songs, so each time they are played live, they may sound a little different to a trained ear. Not Lynyrd Skynyrd. In their formative years, they practiced from early morning until late evening in a small hut near the swamp, deep in rural Florida.[16] They just played and played and played until they could perform their songs in their sleep.

Their songs were the ultimate creative experience. Ronnie Van Zant, the band's main songwriter and lyricist, would ask for ideas, a few chord licks, anything to kick the day off. Once they had something from the guitarists, bass player, or keyboardist, he would dream up some lyrics, singing them but never writing them down. He was a masterful poet, but he was also a great listener. There was a lot of experimentation, and when the band lacked self-confidence, they worked together to rebuild it.

They thrived on having a shared purpose and, in the early years of the band, actively pursued continuous improvement in their

---

14 Rolling Stone. *Inside the Lynyrd Skynyrd Plane Crash That Killed Ronnie Van Zant, Steve Gaines and Cassie Gaines.* Rolling Stone, October 20, 2022, https://www.rollingstone.com/music/music-features/lynyrd-skynyrd-plane-crash-1977-ronnie-van-zant-1234618710/

15 *If I Leave Here Tomorrow: A Film About Lynyrd Skynyrd*, directed by Stephen Kijak (Los Angeles: CMT / Passion Pictures, 2018).

16 Markman, Ron. *Lynyrd Skynyrd: Remembering the Free Birds of Southern Rock.* New York: HarperCollins, 2006.

music. Sometimes they would agree to sleep on it and pick it up the following day. Ronnie would ask the band to play it again, and again, until they felt it was just right. Sharing perspectives and taking on feedback to continuously improve was probably the most critical ingredient in helping Lynyrd Skynyrd make it to the top.

Ronnie Van Zant was clearly a leader, years ahead of his time, and he intuitively knew how to get the best out of every member of the band. Upon reflection, Ronnie Van Zant may well have been considered an agile coach in many respects. When writing songs, they started with the most difficult task, coming up with the hook, lick, or melody. Once they had that, Ronnie composed the lyrics. Then they fine-tuned the song, applying lots of trial and error and striving to continuously improve until it felt just right. Finally, they gave it a title.

Internal Auditors can learn lessons from Lynyrd Skynyrd and the late, great Ronnie Van Zant. Be creative and use trial and error as well as experimentation to your advantage. If you get good at something, invest the time to master it and become great at it. Work together as a team to generate ideas, build self-confidence, and embrace continuous improvement. Practice makes perfect.

Coaching in Internal Audit

Everybody can benefit from coaching, and while there are many different coaching styles, it is the journey that coaching provides us (both as individuals and as teams) that helps unlock value. The value from coaching will come gradually and be realized incrementally.

Continuous improvement is a powerful tool to include in your Internal Audit toolkit, as the cumulative impact of many small changes can be transformational. To help you understand coaching in Internal Audit, I have developed the Rogers Wheel of Internal Audit Leadership Competencies, which contains behavioral keys to support your coaching journey. In the next chapter, we will explore each of these Internal Audit 'must-have leadership skills' in more detail.

Rogers Wheel of Internal Audit Leadership Assurance Competencies

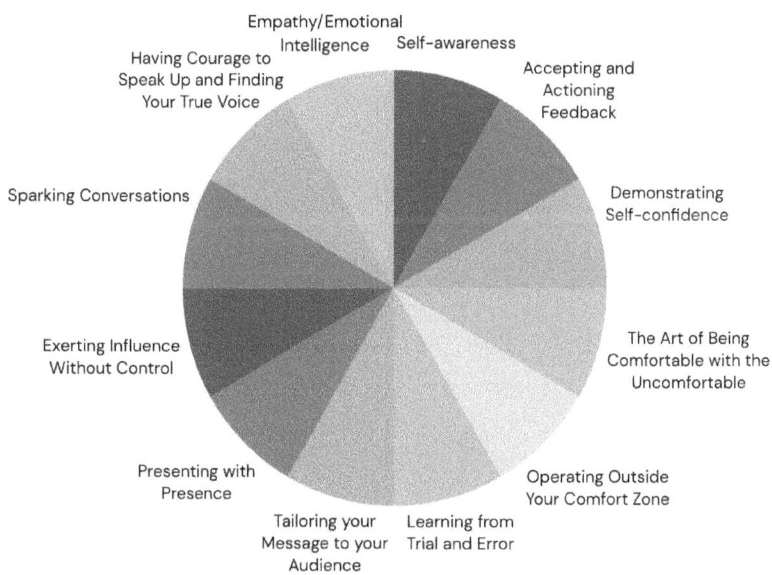

Recap of Key Learnings in this Chapter:

1. Leadership is much more than being the senior person in a team or being the boss. Leadership requires an open mindset and a deliberate focus on helping your team members learn, grow, and thrive.

2. Few leaders are naturally born; coaching is a critical leadership competency and foundational to becoming a great leader in any team, including Internal Audit.

3. Leadership competencies vary, so review those outlined in The Rogers Wheel to identify your strengths and plan how to address weaknesses and blind spots. No pain, no gain.

Chapter 4

INTERNAL AUDIT
ASSURANCE LEADERSHIP AND BEHAVIORAL COMPETENCIES

Like great auditors, great musicians such as Ronnie Van Zant, Rory Gallagher and Lemmy demonstrate that integrity about consistency, purpose, and tone matter more than applause.

To be an effective Internal Audit leader today, you must invest in a broad array of competencies to sharpen your behaviors and character. Being good at just a few things is probably not enough to earn your way to the top of your Internal Audit function. Chief Audit Executive roles can be complex, requiring a deft hand to navigate tough stakeholders, emboldened management, and the delivery of key messages that resonate and lead to action.

Many of us who are, or have been, in the CAE seat understand this well. It is not a role for the faint-hearted. We hold the power of the pen and have a corporate voice that is actively listened to.

Our role, in many respects, is to be the conscience of the organization, adjudicating and advising in practical terms, on the outcomes we have observed and tested. Furthermore, we are well-positioned to highlight plausible risk scenarios that we can foresee. Let us explore the top dozen leadership and behavioral competencies that all up-and-coming Internal Audit leaders should look to master. The Rogers Wheel of Internal Audit Leadership Competencies is not an exhaustive list, but it is a practical roadmap to consider as you plot your path toward future success.

The Rogers Wheel of Internal Audit Leadership Competencies Internal Audit Leadership Competency Number One: Self-Awareness

The first step in coaching is being self-aware. Self-awareness requires reflection and an open mind. Some of us do this naturally, consistently reflecting on meetings and call outcomes: how did that go? Did we communicate our points or message clearly? What could we have done better or differently to achieve a better outcome?

Some Internal Auditors may struggle with self-reflection. Why, you might ask? If you have a perfectionist bent (many Internal Auditors do), then you may find yourself in pursuit of thoroughness, completion, technicalities, and details. Instead, you would be better served focusing on bigger-picture outcomes such as value relevance, others' perceptions, and clarity of communication.

In an Internal Audit sense, our success is often driven by how we, and our work products, are valued and perceived by our stakeholders. We can take pride in our work and the mechanical aspects supporting it, but we must always step back to reflect on the big picture if we want to understand our context and strive for improvement.

Be more self-aware and reflect on the outcomes achieved, good, bad, great, or indifferent. Ask yourself (and teams can do this too): What did I or we do well? Where did I or we disappoint or miss the mark? For the latter topics, keep asking why to get closer to the root cause or causes. For example, root causes of poor meetings or audit outcomes that resonate with me as a Chief Audit Executive include:

- Lack of preparation, including clarity on target outcomes
- Insufficient technical knowledge or lack of credibility
- Lack of anticipation (failure to prepare for the other side of the argument)
- Poor communication, struggling to convince management of our points
- Poor support for our points or unclear examples
- Failure to connect with management, coming across as adversaries instead of partners
- Failure to handle management pushback effectively
- Lack of presence or demonstrated interest

Try to reflect on key meetings and calls for a week or two. Spend five minutes jotting down great, good, indifferent, or bad outcomes. Reflect on why. Developing this rhythm will really help you become more self-aware and identify areas for improvement. Further, get into the habit of asking for feedback regularly.

Internal Audit Leadership Competency Number Two: Accepting and Actioning Feedback

Feedback is a gift.

Every internal auditor can increase their relevance and value by seeking and acting on honest, well-intended feedback.

Most of us view asking for and providing feedback as part of the dreaded year-end performance evaluation process. Feedback, however, is only useful if it is provided close to the specific event or meeting, and it must be well-intentioned, honest, and candid when needed. As Internal Auditors, ask your clients, managers, peers, and team members for feedback. It should be relatively frequent and informal. Make it a habit, a good habit.

One ritual I will share is making my son breakfast some mornings (my menu items are quite limited, chocolate chip pancakes or scrambled eggs). As I put the plate on the table in front of my son, I always ask him to give me a score out of ten. My scrambled eggs normally get a nine or a ten, sometimes even a twelve. I am the egg fluff maestro in our house. My pancakes do not fare so well, maybe a seven or an eight on a good day, but my wife has that department covered. Indeed, one day I accidentally used my wife's gluten-free pancake mix and received a one-out-of-ten, along with loud verbal feedback along the lines of "this pancake sucks!"

My son's feedback was right. I am much better at making scrambled eggs than pancakes. Unlike my wife, I tend to burn the latter, not knowing when to flip the pan and perhaps not having the right consistency in my batter. We joke about it all the time, but his feedback is valuable. I now watch my wife and ask how she makes such perfect pancakes. It turned out I had the pan too hot, my batter was not thick enough, and I was too stingy with the chocolate chips. Who knew?

When you ask others for feedback, you immediately signal that you care and value their opinion. That is a good thing, especially with management stakeholders. So do not wait until the end of the audit, or worse, year-end. Ask for feedback every sprint or after every phase of your audit if you are following a traditional audit methodology. Be informal. Listen with an open mind.

Have fun with it if you can; sometimes a bit of self-deprecation or humor can be the catalyst that helps you see or feel the need to change. Draft some high-level actions, but do not dwell on them too much. Your gut reaction or initial thoughts are probably the right ones in terms of what and how to change.

Be systematic about making small improvements, and over time, you will position yourself well for growth and promotion as your maturity shines through. Sometimes you should ask a trusted peer or manager to observe you in a key meeting. Ask them to be objective and focus on your best traits as well as areas you need to reflect on. Coming from a trusted source and being initiated by you, such feedback will help you grow for sure.

Internal Audit Leadership Competency Number Three: Demonstrating Self-Confidence

Rock stars are real masters of this leadership competency as they settle their nerves and take the stage and command the band and show, night after night. Think David Bowie or Freddie Mercury, they had the wow factor in droves. Self-confidence is a great trait for an Internal Auditor to have. Believe in yourself, your value, your impact, and your worth. Being an Internal Auditor can be a very tough role. As objective professionals, our core responsibility is to assess risks, processes, and controls to identify weaknesses and opportunities for improvement.

In many Internal Audit teams, we may review five or six completely different business areas in a single year, requiring us to move rapidly from basic fact-finding mode to identifying and describing areas for enhancement. By design, the rapid and repeated learning curve required is a challenge.

For me, self-confidence was never about having all the answers or being better than everyone else. It was about being reasoned, applying critical thinking, and asking others for their views or perspectives. Knowing where to get a good answer or unique insight is a useful skill in and of itself. And with the recent advent of ChatGPT[17] and other artificial intelligence tools, there is no excuse for Internal Auditors not to be able to find out what 'good' or 'great' looks like.

Equally, having facts to present and discuss (case studies and evidence rather than hunches or assumptions) helps. Being flexible is also important. We should take pride in our work and look to help the business thrive. That is central to the role of Internal Auditors, even if we do not often describe our jobs in that way.

Being humble is also essential. Let us be honest, few of us have much time for people who are cocky and full of themselves. Being self-confident also means being open to others' viewpoints, especially if they are more experienced or expert than you are. This is worth keeping in mind, as self-confidence is also about being reasonable. For Internal Auditors, self-confidence may show up in our written work products, testing results, issues, reports, insights, presentation skills, and the ability to master brevity and impactful delivery.

The key to improving self-confidence is being prepared and practicing while seeking out new opportunities and taking on challenges, even if you feel like you are swimming in the deep end.

One partner at Price Waterhouse, I recall, used to devote a lot of time to practicing his presentations and speech delivery. If you walked past his office early in the morning, you might see him through the glass panels adjacent to his door, seemingly talking

---

17 *ChatGPT* is a generative artificial intelligence chatbot developed by OpenAI and launched in 2022.

to a picture on the wall. He was practicing his message delivery repeatedly until he felt confident enough, with speech in hand, to just speak to his points. I would say this partner was among the best public speakers I ever come across. He was articulate, well-prepared, had great intonation, and was impactful. He communicated his points succinctly, and it was clear he was well-prepared. Quite 'Ronnie Van Zantish,' upon reflection.

Practice makes perfect, and it will improve your self-confidence. New challenges tend to make most of us nervous to some extent, me included. Yes, I have had a few decades of experience working on Wall Street and beyond, but I still get nervous.

The best way to calm yourself is to be well-prepared. Always devote time to thinking about the opposing arguments and views that may come up in a group setting. Taking time to consider the other side of the argument is a great way to gain a perspective you may have missed. It does not mean your position is wrong, but it prepares you better if a different point of view is expressed.

Have a view and express it, but equally, hear others out and reflect on valuable input or suggestions. Self-confidence is not about getting your way or your idea over the line; it is about having positive energy and engagement to help your organization and team progress.

Internal Audit Leadership Competency Number Four: The Art of Being Comfortable with the Uncomfortable

This is a hard one, but it is rooted in the belief that we only learn from our mistakes and failures. If you polled the most successful business leaders or entrepreneurs, many would readily admit they failed spectacularly three or four times before they succeeded.

Their ultimate success is often attributed to the life lessons they learned from failure. Failure can be a good thing; it teaches us what not to do and helps us redirect our efforts toward pursuing other strategies and approaches. 'Fail fast' is a phrase you hear a lot these days.[18] For Internal Auditors, it is no different.

The first thing you often must deal with when you become a Chief Audit Executive is the reality that, no matter how good you are, you cannot control everything, and you are very reliant on your team members to do great work. We can positively influence and suggest strategies, but it will be the team that creates success, and every now and again, a failure. Do not panic. That comes with the territory of being an Internal Audit leader. No matter how big or nasty the failure is, somewhere there will be an opportunity for Internal Audit to pivot and turn a negative into something a bit more positive.

I recall one such incident when I was head of a UK audit team, and a big error was found in the financial statements. As you can imagine, there was much consternation in the Audit Committee when it was time to go over the issue. Various first line and second line management representatives explained what had happened and over what period the error had built up. It was a harrowing tale of woes and missed opportunities. Of course, eventually, the question was posed by the Audit Committee Chair: "*And where was Internal Audit?*" Not a particularly comfortable place to be that day, I can tell you.

While we had not audited that functional area recently, the incident allowed us to help shape some combined work with the other assurance functions. We later returned to the Audit Committee with new ways to audit some of the broader risks. It became a joint effort, and the issue turned out to be pivotal, bringing the assurance teams much closer together and far more

18 Ries, Eric. *The Lean Startup: How Today's Entrepreneurs Use Continuous Innovation to Create Radically Successful Businesses.* New York: Crown Business, 2011.

willing to take feedback and direction from each other. Over the next few years, we became Coordinated Assurance Partners, and our cohesive work and impact were greatly appreciated by the Audit Committee and Board. We added much more value than the sum of our individual parts.

The key learning here is that negative feedback for Internal Audit is not necessarily personal. Anybody in front of the Chair of the Audit Committee when a big error is being discussed will be on the receiving end. It is how you react and respond that measures you as an Internal Audit leader. There will be times when the only answer is, "Yes, we need to do better."

Failure is how we progress and learn.

Internal Audit Leadership Competency Number Five: Operating Outside of Your Comfort Zone

For me, this is like being comfortable with being uncomfortable, but perhaps it is more self-driven by Internal Auditors themselves. Proactively placing yourself in an audit or a rotation outside of Internal Audit would be examples of this.

Progressive Internal Auditors look for opportunities to learn new skills and to be exposed to parts of the business they may not normally interact with. I am suggesting proactive differentiation to help you grow on the job while expanding your capabilities and knowledge.

I encourage every Internal Auditor who has the chance to pursue a rotation outside of Internal Audit to see what it is like in the business, where risks are more real and outcomes matter. Internal controls have a place too, but you will probably find that internal controls are the formal manifestation of having very capable business leaders and staff.

In most organizations, certainly all the ones I have worked in, front-line staff and management want to do a great job. They want to work in a great company, do good, ethical business, and make a decent paycheck. There is absolutely nothing wrong with that. I was lucky enough to spend over eight years in various first-line teams in the middle of my career. What I learned from those experiences made me a much more valuable, relevant, and empathetic leader. Do not be afraid to work outside of Internal Audit; it will really help you put internal controls in a broader perspective, and you will gain a lot of respect for management, who are often under great pressure to deliver results.

Experiencing life on the other side of the internal controls fence is not a bad thing at all. When I worked in Strategy and Fixed Income Strategic Client Coverage roles, I truly experienced the need for speed and the pace of business in a securities trading environment. All the people I worked with and supported were exceptionally smart (this was Wall Street, after all), but I learned that having sound internal controls is just one part of a big, complex puzzle. I emerged as a much more commercial and empathetic leader from those first-line roles.

Internal Audit Leadership Competency Number Six: Learning from Trial and Error

To err is to be human, as the old saying goes.

Internal Audit staff will periodically make mistakes in performing their work. That is quite normal and is largely reduced or eliminated by peer and supervisory review procedures, which are standard practices. Being an effective Internal Audit leader requires giving the team space to make mistakes, learn from them, and try new approaches.

Sparking team discussion on possible processes or methodological changes is a good thing, and we used to always have an open mic slot at our team meetings to share new ideas and suggestions. Sometimes value can come from a seemingly small change.

For example, at one former employer all draft audit reports had to be presented to the Executive Team Review Board, and our comments had to be answered. We used to have these sessions every Tuesday and Thursday and required two days' notice to allow us to review reports and add comments. One team member suggested moving the calls to Monday, Wednesday, and Friday. The reason was that if you missed a Thursday session, you lost two workdays and four days until the next scheduled Review Board. Adjusting the schedule helped the team achieve their report issuance metrics. It made perfect sense and improved our reporting results, very simple and very effective.

Trying new approaches to solve problems and increase value-added should be openly encouraged. Staying static only ensures faster irrelevance. When trialing, it is important to state what problem you are trying to fix. Conducting a pilot and measuring results is key. Sometimes we achieve great outcomes and sometimes not.

As Internal Audit leaders, we must openly encourage change in our teams. We must also realize that trials may not realize their full potential right out of the gate, but perhaps enough value is yielded that we can all get behind it. More value will come from practice and improved know-how, so my suggestion is to embrace and adopt change as a default position and only revert to the status quo if results and feedback are negative with little hope of correction.

In our team, we used to have a global Change Board where team members debated possible process and methodology changes.

When those ideas were broadly supported, they would proactively seek input and approval from the Executive Team to commence a pilot. This was very grassroots-oriented and served to empower the team. Bottom-up change is often easier to sell than top-down initiatives, since the team drives the former. Progressive Internal Audit teams should aim to strike the right balance between the two.

Internal Audit Leadership Competency Number Seven: Tailoring Your Audience Message

In group settings, these skills can make or break you. You must tailor your message and style to your audience. Practice is critical. I spent countless hours the day or two before the Audit Committee meeting honing my message delivery. I found writing the key points and ordering my script helpful. For example, my script might say:

Page One

Mention the overall audit plan status and metrics. Deliver the key message(s).

Highlight audit p and issue q.

Take the rest of the page as read.

Page Two

Highlight the rationale for the two proposed audit plan changes.

Page Three

Explain the scope change to audit f.

Page Four

Outline the key risk themes to be covered in our proposed quarterly audit plan.

Mention audits x, y, and z and how they relate to the organization's key risk themes alignment.

Ask the Audit Committee members for their feedback.

Answer their questions.

Request audit plan approval.

Pages Five to Eight

Take materials as read. Any questions?

As you can see, this is a checklist for myself. Almost every time I spoke to an Audit Committee, I did not need the punch list but having it gave me confidence as I delivered each point. Being prepared gives you confidence.

Also, anticipating tough questions is critical, so spending time reflecting on how to respond to specific questions helps to sharpen your focus. Having presence is not about being big or loud. Presence, for me, is about credibility, knowing your material, being authentic, keeping your audience interested, and making points that resonate. So again, practicing and researching topics is essential. It is also important to be audible, to speak clearly and loudly enough. A faster-paced delivery helps to keep the audience interested. Avoid being slow, lethargic, or monotone.

Practice in your team meetings and informal settings. Ask a colleague to observe you and give you feedback on your intonation, clarity, message delivery, and the quality and readability of your slides.

Internal Audit Leadership Competency Number Eight: Presenting with Presence

I have a loud voice, and I tend to speak reasonably quickly. Those are good traits to have when presenting because you will keep your audience engaged. We can all relate to there being nothing worse than a slow, monotone presenter. A minute into the presentation, your mind tells you this is going to be painful.

Speed is just not their thing, unfortunately. You find yourself looking around the room to see if anyone is still paying attention. In larger sessions, half the room will probably take a bathroom or coffee break, and some may not return until the next speaker is up.

Other presentation styles to avoid include the whisperer, when they take the stage and start delivering their message, you feel as if you have suddenly lost your hearing. "Get me a hearing aid fast!" The perfectionist is next on my list. You know that presenter with slides packed in tiny font who rarely gets past the first couple of slides because they get bogged down in fine details. Actively squinting and contemplating a visit to the optician, you switch off, hoping they might at least make some sense given how detailed their slides were. Not good.

If you have avoided these types of presenters in your career so far, you have been lucky, and it might be time to buy some lotto tickets.

And we have saved the best for last, the reader. The reader takes the stage and literally reads aloud every word on the page. You feel like it is kindergarten all over again. Story time, but without milk and cookies.

Hope you are having fun recounting various presenting encounters that make you think there must be a better way. Presenting with confidence requires four key steps:

Step One: You must know your content cold. Practice and time your delivery. Know what to say, the order to say it in, and how to say it. I time myself so I know which slides to dwell on and which to just touch lightly. Being prepared is half the battle. Being authentic and sharing nuggets of wisdom with your audience that perhaps are not written down on your slides keeps them interested.

Step Two: Your slides should have a few big bullet points and one key message. Using an image on one side helps keep text down. Use a large font (size 16, 18, or 20). Keep your bullets short, ideally one line, and end with a key takeaway in a larger font.

Step Three: Speak reasonably quickly. A fast-paced delivery keeps the audience engaged. People need to focus a bit to absorb your message, and that is what you want. Use your own words and phrases to deliver the essence of your slide content and key points. Do not read the slides verbatim. Offer context or examples, be lighthearted if you can, and add humor. I often provide examples of things that did not go quite to plan.

Step Four: Always allow time for questions and state your preference upfront. For me, it is often better to take questions at the end, otherwise you risk losing your train of thought or being sidetracked by tangential questions. Keep your answers short and avoid running on too long. If you have ten to 15 minutes, try to get through five questions. Maintain the pace and manage those who try to slow you down or ask irrelevant questions.

If your presentation is less formal, for example, to peers or your manager, you can either indicate that you will take questions at the end or after each section. It depends on how well you know your audience. For Audit Committees, Boards, and conferences, take questions at the end unless a committee member signals otherwise.

When answering questions, keep your responses concise and resist the urge to showcase everything you know. Be honest. If a question requires further research, say so and commit to following up later. Do not wing it or make things up, as doing so will only cause you to lose credibility immediately. Always retain your integrity and be yourself.

Internal Audit Leadership Competency Number Nine: Exerting Influence without Control

It sounds like the perfect world, helping management and the board see your point of view without all the usual formality that comes with Internal Audit products. Our soft side can at times be as effective, or even more so, than our formal reporting. The key is trust. You must be trusted, and you must be credible with your audience.

A few keywords come to mind here:

- Mindset
- Insights
- Feedback

- Flexibility and optionality
- Experience
- Informal audit cycle
- Solutions

I once attended an offsite overseas where our keynote speaker, a very enthusiastic presenter, advised us not to think outside the box but to think outside the building! Open minds create value.

As Internal Auditors, we must project forward-looking thinking and ideas. To be influential requires mastery of the informal. We auditors are great at formality, but for many, informality is not their strength. We must change that. Sell your ideas, the possibilities, the dream. Everyone loves great ideas, even those coming from the third line of defense.

Do the heavy lifting by being prepared and challenge yourself to pose ideas and questions in the future tense. Have a vision for your clients. Help them see success through changes in risk management practices and sound internal controls. Help them anticipate change, and you will have positioned yourself and your team as great sparring partners and trusted advisors.

Internal Audit Leadership Competency Number Ten: Sparking Conversations

Great Internal Auditors are masters at selling ideas and providing options to their stakeholders and clients.

If you express a strong view too quickly, you may feel compelled to defend it excessively. Conversely, if you contribute little or nothing to a group conversation, you risk being forced into accepting the views of others, even when your instincts tell you there might be a better way to provide assurance.

In our roles, it is important that we spark good conversations around risks, internal control effectiveness, and all aspects of the commercial enterprise. For me, an effective way to spark conversation is to offer key topics for discussion and feedback. In group meetings, it takes skill to ask for and obtain meaningful input.

Some of the best ideas and suggestions often go unsaid because some people are introverted and may not feel comfortable speaking up, especially if there are senior leaders in the room or on the call. It is not unusual for people to go into survival mode and stay quiet; I have observed this, many times.

After a key meeting, invariably, someone will come up afterward with a flash of brilliance, but at that point, it may be too late to change opinions or the direction of travel. So, ask questions, and if necessary, call on specific people to share their views. Sometimes that is all it takes to spark great conversation and the sharing of ideas in team meetings.

Be open-minded, and if you sense someone is a bit introverted, make sure you have their back. It is easy to add direct support, for example: "Building on Mary's insight, we might want to consider trying strategy X or Y on this audit. What do you think? Would anyone suggest we change our approach or focus? How?"

For conversations in an online or in-person group setting to be useful, it is important that we do not keep hearing from the same few people. You know the type, extroverts who are loud, brash, and love to hear themselves speak. Despite giving them a bit of a hard time, I would probably put myself in that group. I have always been very extroverted and never afraid to chime in with my views. However, over the years, I have learned not to grab the mic straight away. Being in listening mode is a good thing for me.

Equally, some people simply cannot seem to get to the mic, not because they do not have something valuable to say, but because they have an inner politeness that prevents them from interrupting or timing their entry into the conversation just right. I always seemed to be a fraction of a second faster to the mic, or perhaps once I started to speak, I did not instinctively give way to another speaker, though many times I did, just to spark the conversation.

Do not be afraid to get to the microphone first or fast. If you struggle with this, practice active participation. Getting to the mic is half the battle. Once you do, make sure you contribute positively and make good points without overextending your remarks. Great Internal Auditors do not always know the answers right away, but they tend to identify potential issues and options for solutions, and they tend to know where to go, or whom to go to, to resolve key open questions.

Internal Audit Leadership Competency Number Eleven: Having Courage to Speak Up and Finding Your True Voice

A critical skill for Internal Auditors is to find their voice and speak up, candidly describing issues or weaknesses and pivoting to solutions. Without a voice of reason and sound reasoning, we would struggle to have an impact on our organizations.

At times, speaking up is hard; it is not unusual for Internal Auditors to feel that the Audit Committee, Boardroom, or Executive Management Committee meetings can be intimidating. We are often bearers of bad news; poor risk and control outcomes from our testing and data analysis, or poor risk culture practices and observations, are not necessarily what everybody wants to hear. But if your voice is a voice of reason, and you express issues in candid, commercial terms that people can relate to, you might find the process of speaking up a bit easier.

We should always strive to be diplomatic in our wording, using terms that are neutral in tone and matter of fact rather than sensationalist. This is especially true in how we write audit issues, report summaries, and conclusions. Our words should be our own, objective yet mindful of tone.

For me, our audit reports were always about helping management help themselves. I always wanted the business to plug gaps and weaknesses, to grow and be more successful. If I happened to play even a small part in that (say two percent or three percent), whether by improving control effectiveness, risk awareness, or margins, I would consider myself worth my weight in gold.

History often teaches us that courage, integrity, and empathy are not traits exclusive to Audit Committees or boardrooms. They are universal virtues seen in leaders, musicians, and rebels alike. We will explore a few examples of musical voices that either challenged the status quo, or that were unique, empathetic and impactful, involving punk rocker John Lydon, his band The Sex Pistols, and Blues guitar legend Rory Gallagher.

A Pistol Speaks Up and a Hurt Nation Wished They Had Listened

Johnny Lydon, also known as 'Johnny Rotten,' the iconic frontman from the infamous punk band The Sex Pistols, is probably not someone Internal Auditors would typically think they could learn anything from, other than what not to do. Yet, if you dig a bit deeper into his character and history, you will find that Mr. Lydon is not so rotten after all. He was one of the fathers of the punk rock movement in the mid-seventies and liked to challenge the establishment and promote rebellion in pursuit of social justice.

Scrawny, scruffy, and with bad teeth, he was no 'oil painting', as they say in the UK. But he did have two great attributes in abundance: courage and the willingness to speak up. Most of the time, his well-chosen words delivered stinging lyrics and social commentary or shocked his audience, but he also showed journalists that he was, despite his menacing looks, an intelligent and articulate public speaker.

In one interview with the British Broadcasting Corporation (BBC), which was recorded but not aired in the late seventies, John Lydon told BBC management that they had a very famous presenter on their payroll who, in his words, was "up to all sorts of seediness" and should be investigated. He was referring to Jimmy Savile, and BBC management was all too aware of that. Soon afterward, John Lydon, not Jimmy Savile, was banned from the BBC for various trumped-up reasons, likely his reward for being a whistleblower and perceived threat to a then-beloved figure of the British establishment.[19]

Outside the UK and Ireland, Jimmy Savile was not well known, but from the late sixties well into the new millennium, he was among the most famous radio and TV personalities in the UK. He was wealthy and appeared to do tremendous good for society, raising tens of millions of pounds for charity and being knighted by the Queen. So trusted was Jimmy Savile by the British establishment that he was allowed to personally drive the Queen and Prince Philip in his gold Rolls Royce around the hospital grounds he had helped fund. He was iconic, part of the furniture of UK television, and seemingly untouchable.

After his death, hundreds of his victims came forward, revealing that Jimmy Savile had led a double life for decades. He was accused of committing hundreds of horrendous crimes (too

19 BBC Archives. Interview with John Lydon (BBC Radio 1, 1978). Originally recorded in 1978, first aired in 2013. London: British Broadcasting Corporation.

graphic to dwell on here), using his clean public image to mask his predatory behavior.[20]

Britain was a nation in shock, reeling from the depth and breadth of Savile's crimes. When the Public Inquiry Tribunal completed its investigation, Britons could only reflect on the lost opportunities to stop, apprehend, and convict him while he was alive. John Lydon had been right all along, having gone on record decades earlier trying to change minds at the BBC. A nation reflected sadly on the missed opportunity.

So, what can we Internal Auditors learn from John Lydon?

Have courage and do not be afraid to speak up and make your points well. Choose your words carefully and stand up for what is right. Others may have different views but let your words be your words and their words be their words. Demonstrate integrity, stick to your professional principles, and do not be fooled by superstar syndrome or groupthink.

Internal Audit Leadership Competency Number Twelve: Being Empathetic and Having Emotional Intelligence

Many people might suggest that the role of the Internal Auditor is to be tough, uncompromising, hard-nosed, and independent, to never trust anyone, not even the board members and senior

20 Dame Janet Smith. *The Dame Janet Smith Review: Report of the Investigation into Matters Relating to Jimmy Savile at the BBC*. London: British Broadcasting Corporation, 2016.

executives we work for. Historically, we were often viewed more as cops than advisors. In many respects, a few decades ago, there might have been some truth to that assertion.

When we relied on manual files and ledgers, our work required far more vigilance and person-to-person assessment. Back then, data analysis was limited, and analytics were rudimentary. Without the modern technology we now take for granted, our judgments relied heavily on human evaluation. Could the wool be pulled over our eyes? How much could we trust the people whose work we were reviewing?

To be honest, a little empathy goes a long way. My description above is for historical contrast, but in practice, both as a public auditor and an Internal Auditor, I always had empathy for the management and staff I worked with. Being reasonable, flexible, and approachable always helped me connect with my auditees. They were often going through year-end or juggling other projects that competed for their time.

Sometimes, certain times of day worked better, quieter, and less pressured. Other times, grabbing a coffee or pulling up a chair to talk through a challenge helped build understanding. Being flexible on deadlines and turnaround times (within reason and without jeopardizing the overall engagement or audit timing) will always work in your favor.

Sensing and understanding how someone feels is an important perceptive skill for auditors. Timing is everything, and it is important to put auditees at ease. If your process and controls walkthrough feels disjointed or produces many manual errors and rework, have some empathy for the people involved. It could well be that they are doing a great job under difficult circumstances. If so, acknowledge that openly.

A challenging audit can help management prioritize investment where needed. If the issue is procedural or data-driven, Internal Audit can help there, too. There is always value to be gained from an objective opinion.

I recall one Internal Audit many years ago when I had to review our broker-dealer's adherence to the Customer Reserve and Segregation Rule, SEC Rule 15c3-3.[21] For us, it was an annual required audit. This time, though, it was me who needed empathy. The system used to calculate adherence to the formula had changed since the prior audit, and I had inherited a prior-year file that was, as my grandfather used to say, "as useful as a bag of hammers." The rules were complex and required expert knowledge of securities processing and clearing practices, which I did not possess.

Luckily, the operations experts (Mike and Kevin) were keen to see a thorough audit of the new setup, and they helped me out. Every afternoon, we grabbed coffee and chatted through the new logic. Learning by osmosis, it all came together, and soon I was speaking their unique 'customer reserve formula' language. I truly appreciated their empathy, and it allowed me to perform a much better audit because I finally understood what I was doing and why the new system had been implemented. It was a win-win situation.

Being empathetic improved the quality of the audit, and empathy works both ways. When Internal Audit shows that it cares, we are trusted more, and management will engage with us more openly. When we care, we build stronger relationships, and our work has a greater impact.

Are You the Greatest Internal Auditor No One Has Ever Heard Of?

Admittedly, this is a strange question to pose to any Internal Auditor. If your answer happens to be yes, then you probably need to start a podcast or write a book to share your Internal

21 Securities and Exchange Commission (U.S.). *Rule 15c3-3, Customer Protection – Reserves and Custody of Securities.* Code of Federal Regulations, Title 17, §240.15c3-3. Washington, DC: Government Publishing Office, current through 2025.

Audit wisdom with the rest of us. We all strive to be professional; however, few of us would ever claim to be the greatest of all time. The real question is how we are perceived as Internal Auditors. Empathy builds connection but influence also depends on visibility. Once you've learned to care and connect, the next step is ensuring your voice and impact are recognized.

The Greatest Guitarist You Never Heard Of?

Rory Gallagher, a legendary blues-rock guitarist from Ireland, is often tagged as 'the greatest guitarist you never heard of.' This, in my view, is unfortunate because many have said he was possibly among the greatest guitarists ever, and I would unashamedly agree. He was a masterful acoustic guitarist, electric guitarist, slide guitarist, mandolin player, saxophonist, harmonica player, and singer. He was the frontman and lead guitarist for the rock band Taste, a power trio in the late sixties and early seventies, before going on to a long and successful solo career.

Known for both his soulful blues and blistering electric and slide guitar solos, Rory was a peer of Jimi Hendrix and was, by all accounts, offered spots in Cream, The Rolling Stones, and Deep Purple when their lead guitar roles became vacant in the late sixties and early seventies.[22] Rory graciously turned down those lucrative opportunities, choosing instead to focus on his own music and band. He had integrity and objectivity; he simply did not want to fill someone else's shoes. He had vision and wanted to blaze his own trail.

Rory flew under the radar on purpose. He never released a single aimed at the pop charts, only albums, and he toured almost nonstop. He was a musician's musician and never had any interest in being called a rock star. That said, all the great blues masters sought him out to jam (Muddy Waters, Albert Collins,

---

22 Muise, Dan. *Gallagher, Marriott, Derringer, and Trower: Their Lives and Music.* Bloomington, IN: iUniverse, 2002.

Albert King, and many others). He simply loved to play live, and he was a fantastic showman.

In Ireland and across Europe, he is a legend, soft-spoken, humble, and down to earth. He influenced countless bands in the seventies and eighties. Rory chose his own path; fame and fortune meant little to him. He did not need a number one song to be impactful.

One band that opened for him recalled that when they got paid, they noticed the fee was much higher than agreed. When they asked why, Rory's brother and manager Donal explained that Rory had heard the band had fallen on hard times (a planned break-out tour in support of a well-known band had just been cancelled) and Rory just wanted to help them out. He had great integrity, doing the right thing when nobody was looking. I am proud to say I saw Rory Gallagher perform live once, and he was the greatest guitarist I have ever seen. He could make that beat-up Fender Stratocaster guitar wail and sing like nobody else.

In the documentary *Ghost Blues: The Story of Rory Gallagher,*[23] one story stands out. In the mid-seventies, Rory and his band opened a New York show in Central Park for Aerosmith. That night, Rory was on fire. The audience demanded three encores (unheard of for an opening act[24]), and chants of "RORY, RORY, RORY" echoed well into Aerosmith's third song. Try following that act, even as the headliner.

Rory Gallagher had a clear purpose. He always saw himself as a live performer, a showman. He had a unique guitar voice that

---

23 *Ghost Blues: The Story of Rory Gallagher*, a documentary film directed by Ian Thuiller and released by Capo Records on September 14, 2010. Directed by Ian Thullier. London: Eagle Vision, 2010. The film explores the life and musical journey of Rory Gallagher and includes reflections from many musicians and commentators who knew him well.

24 Rick Beato. 2025. "Aerosmith's Joe Perry and Brad Whitford Talk about Rory Gallagher." *YouTube short*, January 2, 2025, https://www.youtube.com/shorts/NqLLyXy9BOw.

was always heard, always appreciated, and always left audiences in awe. That was his calling card.

So, what can we as Internal Auditors learn from Rory Gallagher?

What personal brand do we have, or want to have? How do we market ourselves and our capabilities? If we do not promote and communicate the value of our work, are we doing ourselves justice in terms of transparency, impact, and value delivery? Anyone who is ambitious (and most of us are, to some extent) should reflect on this and ask: Are we doing a good enough job of self-promotion and professional marketing within our organizations?

Have we found our own voice, a voice that influences management without direct control, a voice of reason and sound risk-based judgment? Do we have an impactful voice that is listened to and respected, just like Rory's Stratocaster?

Huddersfield, Christmas Day 1977

Sometimes just turning up or expressing an informal or unexpected view, or being vulnerable, is all that is needed to demonstrate that we care. Informality can help internal auditors build trust with management.

A regional city in industrial England witnessed one of the greatest examples of empathy and giving back, in modern musical history. A depressed, drab place, Huddersfield was the location to be on Christmas Day 1977 if you were a punk rock fan.

Let's set the stage. At the time, the United Kingdom was enduring a wave of strikes by public sector workers seeking better pay and conditions amid the unrelenting impact of inflation and the oil price shocks from a few years earlier. There was a national firemen's strike over Christmas 1977, and many firefighters and their families felt like Christmas was being cancelled that year. Misery reigned. Money was in short supply, and many young children in firefighting communities across the UK would likely go without Christmas presents. The whole country was struggling, and few seemed to care.

Meanwhile, the UK's best-known punk rock band, The Sex Pistols, were facing their own form of public unrest. Town and city councils, along with concert venues, had banned them from performing and making a living. Earlier that summer, they had a number one hit single, God Save the Queen, which infuriated the British establishment with its anarchic, anti-establishment lyrics and tone.[25]

Despite having the highest record sales in the country that week, the band was erased from the top of the UK Music Charts with a thick black marker line across their name. The timing (coinciding with the Queen's Silver Jubilee celebration) made their exclusion even more pointed. Their rebellious message did not sit well with conservative Britain, and their music threatened the status quo. Reduced to a nomadic existence, they spent their time on their tour bus traveling up and down the M1 motorway, trying to find any venue willing to book them.

When they heard about the plight of the firemen's families in Huddersfield, they decided to hold a benefit concert to raise money for the cause. A suitable venue was booked, and they performed two shows on Christmas Day 1977, coincidentally their last UK performances for decades, as the band disbanded a few months later after a short US tour.[26]

The first show was for the firemen's children, some as young as seven or eight. Not exactly their usual audience. Video footage of the event shows a party with food, cake, and gifts, as well as

25 *Official UK Singles Chart archive (NME/BPI historical notes).*

26 BBC. *Sex Pistols – Huddersfield Christmas Day Concert Footage* (archival film, 1977). London: British Broadcasting Corporation.

free band merchandise for the kids. The Pistols did not have much, but they gave everything they had. Decades later, those who attended as children still recall it as one of the greatest days of their lives.

Even the Pistols themselves were on their best behavior that day. Lyrics were cleaned up to suit the young audience, and even the notorious Sid Vicious was seen smiling and joking. There was laughter, warmth, and connection. The Pistols, often vilified by the media, showed a different side to themselves, empathetic, generous, and grounded. They connected comfortably with the working-class families of Huddersfield because, in truth, they came from similar backgrounds. They were there for these families when others had largely abandoned them. To the firefighters' families, they were local heroes, champions of solidarity and compassion, far removed from their public image at the time.

So, what can we learn from the Pistols and Huddersfield?

Being empathetic and showing that we care is a critical part of how Internal Auditors connect with management and stakeholders. Caring fosters trust. As Internal Auditors, we must care about the business doing well, about preventing mistakes, about management having the earliest opportunity to take feedback on board and about achieving good outcomes beyond the formal audit cycle.

It is vital to care in an unsolicited sense. Find ways outside the audit process to share insights, ideas, and feedback. Showing up informally, with purpose, is often a more powerful value-adding strategy than waiting for formal audits and reviews. Seize informal opportunities with management and key stakeholders to build trust, demonstrate empathy, and add lasting value.

Recap of Key Learnings in this Chapter:

1. Coaching is a great undertaking that will serve to make you better in almost every aspect of your work and career. Some people achieve greatness because they simply have abundant natural talent; the rest of us need coaching to help us get there.

2. Coaching requires self-awareness and reflection. You will not get better until you honestly assess which aspects of your leadership style or delivery are holding you back. Once you face those head-on, you can make changes and start elevating your game.

3. The Rogers Wheel of Internal Audit Leadership Competencies is a useful reference tool to help you focus on key leadership and behavioral traits that will help you thrive.

4. Do not be afraid to try something new and fail. Failure is how we grow in many respects. Learn from your failures, and fail quickly, to position yourself to grow and prosper.

Recap of Key Learnings in this Chapter:

5. How we perform and communicate our work, and how we interact with management, is often as important as what we do. Focus on key behavioral competencies to sharpen your communication effectiveness and enhance your perception and value with stakeholders.

6. Reflect on the lessons from John Lydon and Rory Gallagher; have integrity, speak up on risks that matter to your stakeholders, and find your voice, one that is unbiased and impactful.

Chapter 5

RISK ASSESSMENT AND RISK SCENARIOS—OPTIMIZING THE ALLOCATION OF SCARCE AUDIT RESOURCES

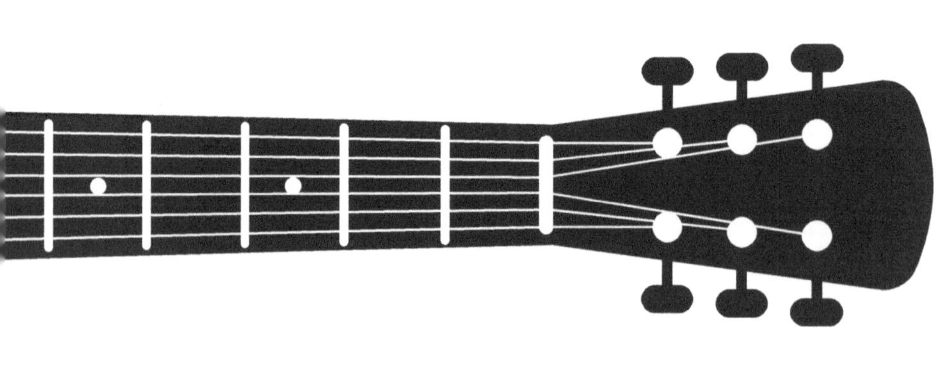

Risk Management or Risk Prediction?

Internal Auditors have never had to demonstrate risk responsiveness to the extent it is required today, and we must be creative and open-minded to take our risk capabilities to a higher level.

Risk management is an integral part of operating a for-profit enterprise. To generate a profit, businesses must take risks with customers, markets, products, and more. Knowing your risk environment and understanding your key risks are important, but effectively monitoring and controlling them is critical to an organization's survival.

Modern Internal Audit teams must devote significant time and effort to ensure they comprehend the current and forward-looking risk environment. While many external resources can help assess the big picture, the best way to ensure Internal Audit maintains a complete and current risk picture is through an active relationship management program with key internal stakeholders, including external audit.

The speed of risk has increased quite dramatically in the past decade or so, given society's technological advancement and continued global integration.[27] Markets, business correlations, and technology dependencies have created great efficiencies but can also amplify risks and create herd effects as organizations face the same challenges simultaneously.[28] Organizational resilience has become part of our business vernacular.

The emergence of artificial intelligence tools and the rapid adoption of AI-driven use cases in businesses will only accelerate the risk cycle in the years to come. So, where should Internal Audit place its chips when it comes to risk management practices to stay ahead of the game?

As we will discuss in Chapter 14, investing time and effort in management relationships is a critical undertaking for Internal Auditors. These regular, calendarized meetings become a key part of any continuous risk management program within Internal Audit. Open and regular dialogue and input from assurance partners in Compliance, Operational Risk Management, and Governance teams can heighten audit knowledge on recent operational or regulatory events and incidents.

These teams, by design, are closer to the first line of defense. Internal Audit should leverage their insights and perspectives while always retaining the right to have a different risk opinion.

Many Internal Audit teams have an annual risk assessment process. These days, it tends to be more of a baseline assessment, often to provide comfort to the Audit Committee and Board that

---

27 World Economic Forum. *The Global Risks Report 2024*. Geneva: World Economic Forum, 2024.

28 Taleb, Nassim Nicholas. *The Black Swan: The Impact of the Highly Improbable*. New York: Random House, 2007.

Internal Audit has a complete inventory of business and systems, ensuring that the starting point of any audit planning cycle is complete and accurate. Traditional audit teams rely heavily on their annual audit risk assessment process. More progressive and agile audit teams devote more time to ongoing awareness of how the organization's risk footprint is changing, looking for the emergence of outsized or unexpected risks to deploy audit resources in real time.

Within one year of adopting an agile auditing approach and shifting to quarterly planning, we felt our audits were more risk relevant and impactful. We identified riskier areas more quickly and could engage more directly with management.

We moved to a quarterly audit planning cycle and supported our risk views with a documented quarterly risk assessment process. This was not the full-blown risk scoring effort typically part of the annual risk assessment process, but rather the gathering of qualitative updates from management and assurance partners so we could document our updated risk views. Changes were centralized in a tool to standardize our assessments by risk theme, priority, region, business division, and other dimensions.

Although we gathered hundreds of data points and insights from quarterly business relationship meetings, only about twenty typically warranted further team discussion. Out of these, three or four updates might trigger a new audit for the quarterly audit plan. All the updates gathered were useful; some were simply to keep on our watchlist radar for coming quarters, while others were valid but less of a priority and were entered into our audit pipeline for revisiting and reprioritization.

Supplementing our qualitative updates from relationships, we also had our data science team run data models to identify operational risk or event trends, growth in business functions or teams, and similar factors. While these data points were always available to us, it was useful to reflect on the key data sets periodically to assess when the data itself might trigger an audit.

AI tools can now connect and highlight insights well, and this capability should be part of every Internal Audit team's planning toolkit.[29] The real value in gathering and processing all these updates was for Internal Audit to have a current risk view and to use that view to ensure our scarce resources were devoted to risks that mattered most to our organization.

As we developed our quarterly 'potential audit list,' it was always useful to get C-Suite input on broader topics, especially thematic audits being considered. Getting management feedback was helpful, particularly to ensure management saw similar value in a proposed audit. Many times, we would go in with proposals for audits A and B, only to come out of the meetings with even better suggestions for audits C and D, reflecting pressing risk issues or management helping Internal Audit shape the right type of audit. Reflecting on current risks with management and sparking conversations with management on these risk, were always worthwhile endeavors for Internal Audit.

Progressive Internal Audit teams continuously monitor the organization's evolving risk landscape. Presenting views on this landscape to the Audit Committee and Board can at times feel overwhelming; almost like a 'boiling the ocean' exercise for Internal Audit to perform and interpret. Completing the audit universe risk assessment is a rite of passage for Internal Auditors and keeping it current is a challenge even for teams that subscribe to a semi-annual or quarterly agile audit planning cycle.

Internal Auditors often reflect on Audit Risk Assessment and Audit Plan questions like:

1. How should you combine the different risk views, bottom up and top down?

---

29 McKinsey & Company. *The State of AI 2024: Generative AI's Next Frontier.* McKinsey Global Institute, 2024.

2. How can we feel comfortable that we are proposing the right audits in the right timeframe?
3. How do we demonstrate that we are largely auditing risks and topics that matter to management and the board and aligned to the corporate strategy?
4. How do we reflect on our audit coverage history while maintaining a forward-looking risk view?
5. How do we demonstrate a logical and risk-grounded audit selection process to our Audit Committee and C-Suite stakeholders and ensure it reflects key risks?
6. Can we use AI-related prompts to identify hidden or connected risk topics that we may be overlooking?

Developing an audit plan game board will help you tell the risk coverage story that needs to be told in your organization. Every organization is different, but most auditors share a focus on identifying critical risk gaps and audit opportunities and communicating them clearly to the Audit Committee.

An audit game board maps the organizational structure (which can be a business or functional listing) to the composite bottom-up risk assessments by risk category and scoring (for example, Red, Amber, or Green) and overlays the top-tier enterprise risks and risk themes. It also reflects past audit coverage, typically three to five years of audits, and can be color-coded to show variations in audit outcomes. Some organizations with mature, coordinated, or integrated assurance functions can also show a composite of Compliance and Operational Risk reviews performed historically alongside audit results, to demonstrate the full assurance perspective.

While a detailed picture to compile, this comprehensive heat map allows Audit to tell the risk story as to why an audit is, or is not, on the proposed plan. There is value in looking back to move forward, especially in highly regulated industries. While our risk views must be forward-looking and grounded in the present in terms of risks, controls, and outcomes, having broader organizational context can be very useful.

You can highlight areas with increasing risk and limited historical coverage, and you can define thematic audits that address key risks at or above tolerance, spanning multiple functions in a single end-to-end review. You can explain decisions not to cover certain areas based on relative risk scores and historical coverage and engage in Audit Committee discussions about areas that were considered but ultimately not included in the current plan. Developing an audit game board will support your Audit Plan and selection logic and encourage risk-oriented discussions with your Audit Committee and management stakeholders.

Anchoring your plan with key risk themes (typically two to four overarching risk themes or enterprise-wide risks that matter most to the Audit Committee and Board in the next 12 to 18 months, such as data quality, artificial intelligence deployment, cyber risk, or business growth and transformation) is a great way to add risk structure to your Audit Plan.

Setting a target resource allocation for these risks helps Internal Audit demonstrate relevance and alignment with the risks that matter most. Not every audit will cover these risks, but a sizable percentage of the Audit Plan (50–70 percent) should. Some audits will focus almost exclusively on these risk themes, while other audits may include one or more objectives that align to them.

Your Audit Committee and Board will appreciate your risk alignment and quarterly updates that demonstrate the results of your risk coverage through audits. Furthermore, Internal Audit can establish and agree on a target resource allocation for each risk theme to optimize focus.

The comparison of target versus actual resource allocation should prompt a richer discussion with the Audit Committee about resources and risk. This allows you to demonstrate how you achieved your intended risk coverage or had to pivot to new risks along the way. The journey and the conversation it sparks with the Audit Committee are often more important than delivering the exact resource allocation proposed.

Internal Audit should always be prepared to react to new or outsized risks or risk events. Using the planning tools above will help tell the story behind any pivots or planning changes and illustrates the risk and value drivers involved.

Key Risk Scenarios for Board Discussion and Challenge, An Exercise Grounded in Murphy's Law?

Organizations generally do a good job outlining their key risks, and having such reports is standard practice in financial services organizations. However, these risks need to be regularly stressed to understand potential failures and to assess the organization's vulnerabilities, monitoring approaches, and ability to manage fast-moving or detrimental changes.

Board Risk and Audit Committees must continue to invest in risk scenario analysis in terms of depth, creativity, correlation of scenarios, and the cadence of holding open, honest, and candid discussions. Board Risk and Audit Committees should remain alert to emerging risks and continuously assess their organization's and people's ability to respond effectively to rapidly changing business environments. As Murphy's Law predicts, what can go wrong will go wrong, eventually.[30]

30 Edwards, A. Murphy. Quoted in Lloyd Mallan, *Men, Rockets, and Space Rats*. New York: Random House, 1957.

Many of us often reflect on personal incidents; it always seems that bad or unexpected things happen at the worst time. You are trying to get out of the house and can't find your car keys. You are in a hurry to get somewhere, and traffic is snarled because of an accident. Murphy's Law feels like an everyday occurrence for many of us. Today, digital transformation and global adoption have connected activities and markets that were far more isolated just a decade or two ago.[31] This heightened global correlation has, in many respects, contributed to the need for developing more complex, integrated risk scenarios.

For example, the modern financial institution needs its Board and management to be adept at assessing positions and potential risk vulnerabilities in such a complex environment. Some aspects of risk are internal to the organization's decision-making (for example, a bank's lending policy and portfolio sector stratification), while others are externally driven (such as inflation and interest rates).

Key risk scenarios should be continuously updated and reviewed at every Board Risk and Audit Committee meeting. Emerging risks, changes to existing scenarios, and the progression of risks should be assessed by risk owners and openly challenged by Board Risk and Audit Committee members. Annual or semi-annual updates on key risk scenarios are not sufficient, given today's speed of risk and the increasing interconnections that make scenarios far more complex.

The waves of globalization, digitalization, and the increased use of artificial intelligence tools will only heighten the need for organizations to be more risk-aware and responsive. Internal Audit must keep pace, providing objective assurance over an ever-changing risk landscape. Looking forward, for many organizations, AI will represent both the biggest strategic opportunity

---

31 International Monetary Fund. *World Economic Outlook: Globalization in Transition*. Washington, DC: IMF, 2023.

(to automate activities, reduce costs and increase productivity) and the biggest strategic threat (the risk that savvy competitors use AI more effectively to outpace and erode business propositions and value).

Board Risk and Audit Committees should demand the highest standards for risk scenario analysis and be willing to rigorously stress key scenarios. Playing devil's advocate and thinking the unthinkable can be a great learning opportunity, as Murphy's Law reminds us almost daily.

Developing and robustly debating comprehensive scenario analyses around an organization's key risks helps Board Risk and Audit Committees and Executive Management teams build confidence that the organization understands its key risks and underlying drivers, both internal and external. Internal Audit must play an active role in ensuring sustained focus on risk scenarios, and the best way to do so is to audit this topic within the organization to ensure that scenarios are forward-looking, regularly updated, owned by qualified management, and complete relative to the organization's structure and footprint. Internal Audit can be a catalyst here and spark conversations on emerging risks and related risk scenarios.

Conducting unannounced mock scenario drills, such as a simulated Board response to a significant cyberattack or other critical risk scenario, is also an excellent way to build organizational resilience and improve board and management understanding of key risks. The risks and response timeframes should be challenged vigorously, given the realities of our digitally integrated world.

Silicon Valley Bank is a case in point; back in 2023, the bank went from boom to bust in just a few days. Unfortunately, it is not uncommon for management teams to believe that crises only happen to other organizations, not theirs. A lack of risk paranoia within an Executive Management team or board should be a cause for concern.

Despite the hundreds of years of collective experience often found on corporate boards, one simple truth remains: you cannot outrun a tsunami once it reaches shore. In risk terms, being open, honest, and candid (and even a bit paranoid) about risk scenarios will help boards and Executive Management teams better prepare for potential catastrophic events. Better preparation is a far safer management strategy than clinging to the corporate myth that they will outperform when a crisis hits. Internal Audit leadership has a role to play here, regularly reviewing risk scenarios and promulgating high standards and discussing critical risks, in relationship meetings with management, within audit reports and Audit Committee updates.

Recap of Key Learnings in this Chapter:

1. To avoid becoming stale, an annual risk assessment process requires continuous evaluation and updates to ensure Internal Auditors maintain a sufficient understanding of the organization's key risks, which are constantly evolving and changing.

2. Internal Auditors should invest in their capacity to gather updates from management and second-line functions to assess key risk changes and remain responsive to risks that matter.

3. Internal Audit should periodically agree with the Audit Committee and C-Suite on the organization's critical top-down risk themes. Individual audits proposed in the audit plan should align with these key risks and risk themes to ensure audit proposals are relevant and meaningful.

4. Risk scenarios should be reviewed by management and the Audit or Risk Committee regularly, prompting open discussion about worst-case scenarios. Internal Audit should audit risk

Recap of Key Learnings in this Chapter:

scenarios as a distinct risk theme to ensure sufficient governance over this critical area and to support organizational resilience.

5. Globalization and digital business models have intensified risk correlations and greatly increased the speed of risk events.[32] Internal Audit should assess whether key risk scenarios are robust enough, using recent debacles as benchmarks for what can go wrong and how quickly.

32 World Economic Forum. *The Global Risks Report 2024*. Geneva: World Economic Forum, 2024.

Chapter 6

AGILE AUDITING, IMPROVING INTERNAL AUDIT RISK RESPONSIVENESS

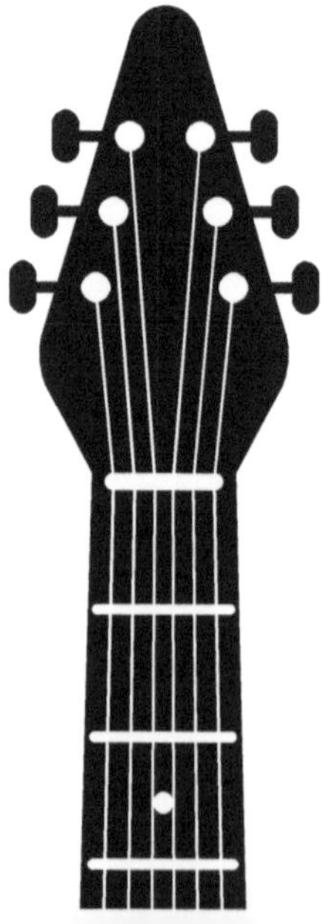

Many Internal Audit teams are adopting agile practices these days or at least contemplating doing so. It sounds daunting, with lots of new terminology to absorb (Sprints, SCRUM Masters, Retrospectives, Product Owners, and so on).[33] However, once you get beyond the lingo, agile is a progressive audit approach that can supercharge your team's impact.

The Audit function where I worked most recently was, and still is, an extremely progressive global team of people. We were on the third extension of our vision, having largely achieved what we had intended to do across a couple of previous multi-year journeys.

Before we adopted an agile audit methodology, our Group Audit Executive noticed that we struggled to stop audits when the right circumstances arose periodically and wrap them up quickly. Our risk responsiveness was not where we wanted it to be,

33 Beck, Kent, et al. *Manifesto for Agile Software Development.* Agile Alliance, 2001. https://agilemanifesto.org/

as we were too flat-footed and too tied to our annual audit plan coverage decisions and commitments. The failings within our annual audit planning cycle seemed to periodically manifest themselves like Banquo's ghost.[34]

Once the Internal Audit train had left the station, it was very difficult to change the timetable or ultimate destination because we were set in our traditional audit ways. Having a typical annual audit plan, like many of our peers at the time, we did not help ourselves by setting a rigid risk coverage expectation twelve to fifteen months in advance. For example, audits performed in Quarter 4 were approved by the Audit Committee in October of the prior year, and this practice felt stale. Risk can change dramatically in a day or a week, never mind in a year.

Like most Internal Audit functions, we took pride in developing our plan and delivering it, and we did not like to change it too much, nor did our Audit Committees like too much change. "We agreed on the plan, so please deliver it," was the sentiment we often encountered among our key stakeholders. We needed to adopt an agile auditing methodology to enhance our risk responsiveness, shorten our planning horizon to keep audit ideas relevant to current risks, and learn how to fail quickly through a much greater focus on value.

Going agile was the path we took to transform ourselves from a progressive but traditional audit function into a forward-looking, risk-responsive team. Implementing an agile audit methodology supported by a quarterly audit plan cycle was transformative for our team and our stakeholders, and it served to further improve our impact and relevance as an assurance function.

As an audit approach, agile is all about adding value and demonstrating continuous improvement. An agile audit methodology enables Internal Audit to stop and periodically assess value coming from the audit work. In its simplest form, for each audit there

---

34 Shakespeare, William. *Macbeth*. Edited by Barbara A. Mowat and Paul Werstine. New York: Simon & Schuster, 2003.

are two logical outcomes: either you keep going and execute an additional sprint in the current audit, or you stop the current audit and start a new one (typically the next most valuable audit in the backlog or pipeline).

With agile auditing, there is much greater emphasis on teamwork and shared objectives, and less focus on the individual auditor. Clearly, each person contributes to the best of their ability, and from a performance perspective, you will have exceptionally strong, good, and weak performers in the team. However, in an agile team, given the closeness, the team becomes more self-directed and self-critical at times, which improves accountability and performance.

When we implemented agile auditing in our global team, we looked at the risk universe through a different lens. It did take some time (six to twelve months) to settle in, as transformational change always does, but it soon became our new normal. As a Chief Audit Executive, I found agile auditing a breath of fresh air and our global audit team found the key principles and practices empowering.

Valuable Agile Audit Components to Embrace

1 – Sprints

Sprints are typically two-week bundles of work (the duration can vary, typically from one week to several weeks, depending on the organization and industry). The time constraint helps to reinforce the ambition of finishing what you start each sprint. Typically, each sprint culminates in a sprint review session with your stakeholders. This meeting is open and transparent and covers the audit work (stories) completed in the sprint, along with exceptions, potential observations, and insights.

This transparency builds trust. In addition, agile teams seek management input on each subsequent sprint in terms of value or areas to focus on (Internal Audit always retains the final call on scoping and testing, to be clear), which is generally seen as helpful and commercial. Our assessment of the value generated by each sprint supports our decision-making: GO (execute another sprint) or NO GO (stop this audit and move to the next most valuable audit in the backlog).

This approach allows Internal Audit to stay responsive to risk. Further, this constant value assessment at the end of each sprint helps reduce low-risk testing, which is a great productivity driver.

The agile approach sharpens productivity as it 'time-boxes' audit work. The traditional approach tends to 'scope-box' audit work, which often results in completion of low-risk testing steps that may add little value to the overall audit outcome.

2 – Sprint Reviews

Sprint Reviews help make Internal Audit teams more accountable for their work and add great transparency to internal audit activity. The discipline of openly recapping the progress made in the last two weeks, outlining test results, observations, and insights, removes the mystery of what is happening in the audit itself. Having a sense of rawness here is not a bad thing because there is real value in reflecting openly on the audit observations with stakeholders.

Many stakeholders have provided feedback to me that this is among the best parts of agile for them; complete transparency and having a voice throughout the audit. I would often note during Sprint Review meetings that management was getting the same audit update on Wednesday that I, as the Chief Audit Executive and agile product owner, had received on Tuesday afternoon. These aspects are critical to building trust with management.

3 – Retrospectives

Retrospectives are shared team learnings after each sprint, facilitated by the Scrum Master. Regularly identifying incremental improvements adds significant value over time and promotes a culture of continuous learning. Once agreed upon by the agile team members, these improvements are implemented in the next sprint.

Retros, as we called them, were always useful. We reinforced what we all felt was working well and identified small, incremental improvements that could be digested and implemented in real time. There are many great collaboration tools available today for Internal Audit teams to share a feedback board and facilitate the gathering of anonymous input, as well as active ranking and grouping of ideas (typically facilitated by Scrum Masters).

4 – Self Managed Teams / Flatter Team Structure

Agile teams must work closely together to achieve shared objectives, which supports a strong teamwork environment. Agile teams meet daily to assess progress and next steps and huddle at the start of each sprint to review resource capacity and size the stories (bundles of work) for the sprint. Value is assigned to each story (similar to an audit sub-objective), helping the team focus first on testing and tasks that matter most.

This increases personal ownership among agile team members and generally supports a flatter team structure with fewer hierarchical layers. In an agile audit team, there is nowhere to hide. If a team member does not progress the work, it becomes apparent during the daily team meeting or call. If there are impediments, the Scrum Master will step in, as might other agile team members. Everyone focuses on the two-week deliverables for the sprint or sprint review, which helps the team remain both productive and responsive to risk.

Out of the box, not everything was smooth sailing. Far from it. We had plenty of reflection sessions to figure out how best to make agile work for our team and organization. If you implement agile strictly by the textbook, you may become frustrated quite quickly. We did. We found that the textbook approach lacked practicality at times, and we needed to fine-tune some of our approaches over time to better fit our global financial services environment. In hindsight, having some guidance from an Internal Audit consultant with practical experience would have been a big help. There are some areas to watch out for and carefully assess when implementing an agile audit methodology in your Audit organization.

Focus Areas for Consideration when Implementing an Agile Audit Methodology

1 – Sprint Planning / Sprint Zero

All audits, even agile ones, need planning and pre-work, particularly if you are executing a data-driven audit. We used to perform quite sophisticated data analysis and develop data hypotheses covering full data populations on almost every audit. This requires sufficient preparation time to gain access to the dataset and ensure it is normalized.

Audits, particularly in large financial institutions, are complex undertakings, and allowing sufficient time for critical pre-audit work is important. This is an area where it is difficult for Internal Audit teams to be fully agile compared with traditional

IT development environments, as audits can vary greatly in terms of risks being covered, technical expertise required, and datasets needed.

As sprints are typically numbered, we called our planning sprint 'Sprint Zero,' and on some large, complex audits, we sometimes needed two of them.

2 – Level of Task Breakdown

Agile methodology expects that tasks be broken down into low-level items. This can be tedious, and the transparency benefit may be outweighed by the added bureaucracy. This is an area where Audit teams can and should draw a reasonable line in the sand. Make it work for your team and apply common-sense rules.

We used a tool called Jira[35] to house all our agile audits, Audits (Epics), Objectives (Stories), and Test Steps (Tasks), and this tool is widely used. However, one drawback became apparent: how to integrate our agile auditing workflow tool with our electronic workpapers system. Our electronic workpaper system lacked portability, and the team members felt that some activities were being replicated across the two systems, such as test conclusions. This is an area to be mindful of to avoid double work.

3 – Organizational / Staffing Hierarchy

We used the SCRUM methodology to support our agile implementation.[36] Within each agile team, the roles of team members

35 Atlassian. *Jira Software*. Accessed November 2025. https://www.atlassian.com/software/jira

36 Schwaber, Ken, and Jeff Sutherland. *The Scrum Guide: The Definitive Guide to Scrum: The Rules of the Game*. Scrum.org, November 2020.

are quite generic, given the flat structure. This can give rise to some friction, as tasks may be performed by auditors with varying levels of experience and different corporate titles.

To be honest, having the title 'Agile Team Member' did not resonate as much with audit staff as being referred to as Senior Auditor, Assistant Vice President, or Audit Manager. So, we kept our organizational titles to help differentiate performance and compensation expectations.

Your approach to reviewing work performed may also need to change, as you may not have the traditional managerial hierarchy within your agile team. We adapted our review process so that peer review was acceptable. The standards of work did not decline, as agile team members all focused on achieving our definition of 'done.' We found that workpapers were reviewed closer to when the work was performed, as the entire team was conscious of finishing what we started, sprint by sprint, to keep our work velocity on target. Any changes you make in this space I would strongly suggest you syndicate with your external auditor firm, lest changes in practices impact their reliance or potential reliance on Internal Audit's work surrounding financial controls.

4 – Moving to a Shorter Audit Planning Cycle Requires Discipline and Focus

Agile auditing has many benefits, as outlined above, and the drive to be more responsive to risks and focus on topics that matter has led many Internal Audit teams to develop a shorter audit planning cycle, moving from an annual audit plan to a semiannual or quarterly audit plan. Adopting a shorter cycle can improve risk coverage focus; however, in practical terms, you need to consider some critical factors.

First, any move away from an annual audit plan is a big change for your Audit Committee and management. You will need to sell the benefits of such a strategic change to the Audit Committee and its Chair. That was a major change, but we had the support of our Audit Committee and its Chair. This may prove to be among the greatest challenges in adopting an agile Internal Audit methodology: the Audit Committee itself. Board members may come from different generations and could be suspicious of the perception that a shorter-duration audit plan allows assurance goalposts to shift.

Of course, proactive demonstrations of risk responsiveness and the ability to cover topical and emerging risk areas more quickly should help your Audit Committee embrace agile as a robust internal auditing methodology.

Management also needs to be on board, as agile audits involve greater management participation and input but much shorter notice periods. In our case, the notice of audits went from twelve months to three months, and in many organizations, this aspect of becoming agile often faces resistance from management. Setting the right tone from the top is critical when adopting agile auditing. For example, having the CEO or Chairman openly support the case for change (generating greater organizational value from audits) will make the transition easier for both management and Internal Audit.

Second, moving to quarterly planning created significant reporting strain on the Audit team, not only pressure to complete audits timely, but also the added burden of developing and presenting the plan for the next quarter to meet strict Audit Committee reporting deadlines. While we are all accustomed to quarterly Audit Committee reports, we can appreciate the work involved in developing the audit plan, selling it to management, and working through any business logistics or timing constraints.

It took us several iterations before we began to develop our quarterly audit planning rhythm. For example, we would develop our quarterly plan a quarter in advance. Our Quarter One audit plan would be developed in October and presented to our Audit Committee in November for review and approval. Our Quarter Two plan would be developed in January and presented to the Audit Committee in February, and so on.

It turned out to be a great improvement for us and allowed us to focus on risks that mattered in the present, rather than what we thought was important twelve or more months earlier under the annual audit planning cycle. We maintained a long list of possible future audits in our Audit Backlog (Pipeline), and this was a living, breathing list of ideas that we added to and reprioritized regularly.

We also had a well-established, calendarized stakeholder meeting structure each quarter, and these meetings were critical to developing credible quarterly audit plans. On balance, this was a big positive part of our agile implementation; however, it required a tremendous effort from the Audit team to stay on top of stakeholder and Audit Committee reporting deadlines.

Agile auditing has the potential to help your team unlock significant value within your organization and is worthy of serious consideration. Larger audit teams have generally been faster to adopt agile, while smaller and mid-sized teams have been a little slower to embrace agile practices. In my view, regardless of size, every audit team can generate value from following agile auditing principles.

A one-person team can be agile, perform work in sprints, hold sprint reviews to ensure transparency, eliminate low-value testing, and be responsive to risk. A couple of years ago, as an independent audit and risk consultant, I performed an external quality review of a risk management and Internal Audit function using agile principles. It was a great experience that delivered value in four sprints while helping my client understand how to adopt the best parts of agile and make them work in practical terms.

There is nothing stopping any traditional Internal Audit department from embracing agile. It is, after all, a value-oriented mindset, and any traditional audit function should be looking to adopt agile, if for nothing else than to help them stay relevant and risk-responsive.

What surprised us most was how quickly transparency built trust. Implementing agile auditing taught us that value is not only in what we deliver but in how fast we learn what doesn't deliver.

Agile internal auditing will continue to evolve as audit cycles shorten even further in the coming years, approaching real-time, AI-enabled auditing. Some very progressive Internal Audit teams may already be well on their way to that north star!

Recap of Key Learnings in this Chapter:

1. Agile audit methodology is a value-oriented approach that helps Internal Auditors become more responsive to risk.

2. Adopting an agile audit methodology is a strategic initiative within an Internal Audit team and requires the support of the Audit Committee, Board, and Executive Management.

3. Agile benefits include greater reporting transparency, the ability to fail quickly, a reduction in lower-risk testing, and improved coverage of key, current risk topics.

4. Agile audit teams typically embrace quarterly audit planning cycles to ensure that proposed audits cover the most relevant risks.

5. Regardless of team size, all Internal Audit teams can adopt agile principles to add value, such as Sprints, Sprint Reviews, and Retrospectives.

Recap of Key Learnings in this Chapter:

6. Agile auditing still requires some audit pre-planning, particularly if testing involves full data sets or populations.

7. Migrating to a quarterly audit planning cycle improves risk relevance and responsiveness, but it requires significant initial effort to establish the right Audit Committee reporting rhythm.

Chapter 7

Integrating Management Risk and Control Self Assessments into Internal Audit Reports

Every audit report tells a story about people, risk awareness, control ownership and culture. Is management open, honest and candid about how it manages its key risks?

Our audit reports, our final products, can be perceived as the culmination of our auditing efforts over a period of weeks or months of work. Audit reports serve several purposes, including being a key stewardship input to the Audit Committee and Board, objectively assessing and testing key risks and internal controls, and highlighting important weaknesses along with solutions to ensure risks are sufficiently remediated.

To be considered a more complete work product, our audit reports should also encapsulate the salient aspects of management's self-assessment gathered on a pre-audit basis. Many organizations operate a robust operational risk framework, and a key part of these frameworks is having a management-led risk and control self-assessment process to help capture remedial actions to address operational risk events and issues.[37]

Our audit reports and our audit opinion are integrated when they reflect both key points self-identified by management and additional points identified through Internal Audit testing. Crafting audit reports in this manner introduces risk culture into the audit reporting process.

In most organizations with formal risk and control governance standards, there is a reasonable expectation that management understands its key risks and has established sound internal controls to monitor and manage these risks. If there is a gap, it is a good thing if management has self-identified it and proactively developed a remediation plan in the enterprise risk system. Management must be given credit for being proactive in this space and being open, honest, and candid.

One Audit Executive I used to work for said candidly, "*The board's expectation is that management is always in control of its risks, and if management cannot control a business, perhaps we should not be in it.*" While this Audit Executive was best described as tough and blunt, the point made about management accountability for risks and controls was a good one. A funny aside, one of my former colleagues was offered a job in a foreign city by this same Audit Executive.

His sales pitch to him on the role went as follows: "*Bernard (not his real name), I will give you three reasons why you should take this job. One: it will pay you 30 percent more money. Two: you will have a nice office looking over the River Thames. And Three: you would be an idiot not to take it!*"

We used to grapple with whether we should ask management for an updated self-assessment immediately before the audit or

37 Basel Committee on Banking Supervision. International Convergence of Capital Measurement and Capital Standards: A Revised Framework. Basel, Switzerland: Bank for International Settlements, 2006.

rely on their most recent quarterly self-assessment logged in our enterprise risk system. You can go either way, to be honest. The latter sets a better expectation that management must take the quarterly self-assessment process very seriously and, in effect, always be expecting an audit. If you use the former approach, the audit itself may be the trigger for management suddenly becoming candid about their risk and control environment. You could say it might be akin to giving a Mulligan (a no-penalty shot retake) when playing golf.

Risk culture is at the heart of this argument, and setting a high bar for management to take responsibility for risk and control assessments and remediation is a good standard. Over the years, we employed both approaches, but in more recent years, we opted to largely rely on the pre-audit management self-assessment within the enterprise risk system. We did allow management to provide an updated narrative for each objective, but they could not raise new self-identified issues immediately before the audit. That seemed like a fair compromise to us.

Sometimes, if the audit was thematic or covered a very narrow scope, we would flex our style and give management the option to provide an updated or stand-alone self-assessment. The key point is that the Audit Committee and the Board should always want to know where management stands and whether they are on top of their risk and control game.

We included management's self-assessment verbatim in the appendix of our report. Typically, it comprised a page of text for each audit objective, and we usually had three to five audit objectives per audit. On a pre-audit basis, management needed to explain how the audit objectives (risk topics) were controlled and outline any self-identified weaknesses and related actions in the enterprise risk system.

They also had to rate the internal control environment for each objective A–D on a pre-audit basis. Our audit testing and results would be referenced to those of management in the right column, and Internal Audit would rate each objective based on our independent testing.

This introduced an interesting risk culture dynamic in terms of whether Internal Audit agreed, partially agreed, or disagreed with management's self-assessment. For example, if management had self-identified some key issues that were being actively remediated, and we had only found a low-rated additional weakness, we would agree with management.

However, if management had only self-identified one low-rated issue, and we found two or three moderate or elevated issues, we would partially agree with management because they had identified some, but not all, important weaknesses.

Occasionally, if Internal Audit found several elevated or high-rated issues that management had not self-identified, we would likely disagree with management's self-assessment, which, in effect, suggested that management was not adequately self-assessing and proactively managing their risks and related controls. While the latter case was a rare outcome (typically, less than 5% of our audits), it did tend to generate much-needed executive focus on risk governance practices and internal control outcomes for that business or function.

This structure was useful because it also allowed us to adjust our audit report conclusions to give credit depending on whether Internal Audit testing or management self-reporting was driving the overall conclusion. For example, if we had an unsatisfactory audit report, but most of the key issues were self-identified by management, we would agree with their self-assessment, and our audit conclusion would report management's self-identified points first.

For our Audit Committee and Board, an unsatisfactory audit report largely driven by management's self-identified weaknesses was not a bad outcome. While there was plenty of remediation work required, management was open, honest, and candid and could demonstrate a good risk culture.

The opposite was also true if we had an unsatisfactory audit report and most of the key issues were identified by Internal Audit. In that case, our audit report conclusion would list weaknesses identified by Internal Audit first, followed by any management self-identified points. We would either partially agree or disagree with management's self-assessment because management was not as open, honest, or candid and could not demonstrate awareness of key weaknesses identified by Internal Audit.

We used judgment in determining our overall ratings, and we also helped deliver training on the importance of open, honest, and candid self-assessments. Indeed, as the Chief Audit Executive, I would pose some review questions on management's draft submissions to help them understand the Group's standards.

This feedback was generally perceived as a positive step for management, given that Internal Audit had seen hundreds of such assessments over the years. For example, I would often ask if the narrative was consistent with their self-ratings; for instance, they might list three open issues against a key audit objective and still choose to self-rate as an A or B when a C was probably more realistic.

Equally, self-reporting one objective as a C did not automatically mean the audit report overall would warrant an unsatisfactory rating. We used judgment to assess the overall internal control environment and results, and we resisted the temptation to overstate the risk. We understood that management must take risks all the time when running a commercial enterprise.

As we operated within a broader Coordinated Assurance Framework, some borderline cases would prompt Internal Audit to have a discussion with our partners in Compliance and Operational Risk. These meetings were always helpful for context and, in my experience, allowed Internal Audit to be commercial and credible in our issues and audit report ratings.

Having a one-page audit report summary is a great thing. Our stakeholders could glean the big-picture outcome (good, bad, or indifferent) and the sources of the key points being raised. Our audit reports were always written in the negative syntax, to promote brevity. We highlighted key weaknesses identified by management or Internal Audit and provided a one-sentence commentary on whether the actions developed by management were sufficient to mitigate the risks. If we had more opportunistic feedback for management, which we called business insights, we might briefly mention them at the end of our audit conclusion or cross-reference a separate report.

Our insights were written as forward-looking opportunities for the business to consider and reflect on further. Our wording here was much more sales-like, positive, and discursive in style, entirely different from our negative and direct audit reporting style. Management did not need to respond with any formal actions, but we always discussed our feedback at the end of the audit with management. We received great kudos from management for generating insights, and it was our compelling insights that helped to position Internal Audit as a catalyst for positive change within the organization.

If we had very compelling insights into a specific audit, with real wow factors, we would look to disseminate the Audit Report and Insights in tandem. Our audit report and insights memos often provided good context when read together. Again, Executive Management and the Audit Committees often appreciated us trying to achieve this level of integrated perspective.

Our auditors also enjoyed providing ideas and softer suggestions, as it made them feel more rounded and valued. It was always worthwhile for us to provide an annual recap of our business insights footprint, including overall thematic opportunities, numbers of insights, and examples that were particularly impactful or resonated with management. This more qualitative and commercial insights product from Internal Audit was very differentiating.

Audit Report Summary Template (Illustration 1 – outlined in the appendix)

While every organization is set up differently and the preferences of key stakeholders may vary, below is an outline of a one-page audit report summary that we found to work well. We purposely laid our reports out in landscape format so they would be easier to digest on iPads and laptops. The topics and headings that worked for our stakeholders included:

Audit Conclusion Paragraph

Outlined our overall opinion on the internal control environment surrounding the function or legal entity and whether it was adequate (or not) to mitigate key operational, financial, and other specific risk categories that might be relevant. Weaknesses highlighted included those identified by Internal Audit or management, listed in the negative. The issues contributing most to our overall rating were listed first.

Conclusion Over Management Risk Culture

We would note whether we agreed, partially agreed, or disagreed with management's self-assessment and often referenced key points included in our audit conclusion and any differences in ratings of audit objectives between management and Internal Audit. We would make a statement on whether the action plans developed by management were sufficient to mitigate the risks identified through our audit work.

Scope

We outlined key scope areas and the use of data analytics. Key exclusions were also noted. We would reference the detailed audit objectives outlined in the Management Self-Assessment section in our appendix.

Background

Typically, this section included a few sentences describing the business, its strategy, key locations, total headcount, recent financial performance or processing volumes, and other key performance indicators and pertinent regulations.

Our audit report summary template had a column representing about one-quarter of the width of the landscape page. In this column, we would present pertinent ratings and risk data, typically as follows:

Report Ratings

Our ratings were all outlined in the right margin of our reports:

Inherent risk rating (Scale 1–4)

Residual risk rating (Scale 1–4)

Key risks from the Group's risk register are covered in the audit, normally the top two or three relevant risks for the unit being audited

Control Environment Rating (A–D)

Management Self-Assessment Rating or Risk Culture Rating, which outlined whether Internal Audit agreed, partially agreed, or disagreed with management's self-assessment.

Remedial actions completion date (the furthest-out date from detailed action plans within the report). This served as a good final check in terms of issues and report ratings. For example, it might be hard to convince the Audit Committee that a low-rated issue would take twelve months to remediate. It is important to reflect carefully on the remediation timeframes associated with audit report issues.

This style worked for our stakeholders because it was direct and got to the point. The one obvious limitation was that there was little room for context or storytelling, and we followed a strict writing style that was always in the negative. Brevity was highly valued, so we kept our audit summaries and report issues tightly worded.

Audit Issue Template

One area to which we devoted considerable training effort was the quality of our audit issue writing. Over the years, we refined our process down to the following rubric, which we followed globally without exception. One tool that was a great writing aid for our auditors was a macro that team members could run against their draft audit reports to highlight conformance with our report writing standards.

Once they ran the macro, they could see their inconsistencies clearly highlighted and address them before sending the draft report for Internal Audit Executive Management review. No doubt artificial intelligence can replace this type of tool, but it proved very effective for maintaining a consistent report writing style and syntax. The audit team loved it, and so did the Audit Executive team.

Issue Title: Had to be written in the negative as a problem statement.

Issue Rating: We had four ratings supported by quantitative and qualitative impact measures: Low, Moderate, Elevated, High.

Issue Description: One sentence outlining who (which function or team) has not done what.

Risk Statement: One sentence, starting with: As a result, something could happen or have happened.

Root Cause(s): One sentence highlighting the root cause factors relevant to the issue.

Support for Issue: short and concise bullet points from our data hypothesis testing or sample testing supporting our issue.

Background: Optional, to include a sentence or two of relevant context.

Action Plans, Due Date, and Owner: We did not make recommendations. All our issues were written as weaknesses, and management had to develop a plan to mitigate the risks identified. Typically, due dates could not extend beyond a year, but once reports were issued, we had a formal Audit Committee reporting process to update any audit issues that were extended, along with the rationale.

Management Self-Assessment Template (Illustration 2 – outlined in the appendix)

Each of the headings below represented a column in a table that formed our Management Self-Assessment. In our audit reports, the Management Self-Assessment section followed our detailed comments section.

Audit Objective: We would list these out; most audits had three to five objectives.

Management Commentary: This was the widest column and detailed how management controlled its key risks. Self-raised issues or operational events in progress were referenced to the Group's Enterprise Risk Management system.

Management's Self-Ratings: This column included a rating for each objective from management, A–D, gathered before the audit.

Internal Audit Ratings for Each Objective: Upon completion of the audit testing, we rated each objective, reflecting on issues identified by both us and management.

Detailed Issues: This was a cross-reference to our numbered audit report comments pertinent to each audit objective. For unsatisfactory audit reports, we would also reference any management self-raised issues contributing to the overall unsatisfactory rating, as these would be subjected to follow-up verification work by Internal Audit upon completion.

As a progressive audit team, we took great pride in performing valuable audits and delivering integrated reports that reflected both Internal Audit and management issues. The cross-check of management self-assessment quality against the actual audit results, both at an audit objective level and in aggregate, introduced an interesting and transparent risk culture dynamic.

Recap of Key Learnings in this Chapter:

1. To provide the Board and Audit Committee with a more holistic view of the risk and internal control environment, audit reports should reflect both Internal Audit issues arising from our review and testing, and issues self-reported by management on a pre-audit basis.

2. It is possible to deliver effective one-page audit report summaries, use the template suggested as guidance.

3. Key differences between management's self-assessment and Internal Audit's testing results may be one indicative measure of the relative risk culture health within the unit being audited. The Audit Committee and Board will likely be most interested in negative surprises, such as management self-ratings that are much rosier than those from Internal Audit, or a lack of self-raised issues from management.

Recap of Key Learnings in this Chapter:

4. Use the audit issue writing rubric to keep audit issues tightly worded (Who / Which Team has not done what). Reporting in the negative helps to promote brevity and keep issues short.

5. Remember, every extra word you use in your audit report simply increases the potential for misinterpretation, misunderstanding, or error. Brevity is gold.

Chapter 8

SHARED VALUES
and Establishing a Coordinated Assurance Framework

Few functions are as respected and as misunderstood as Internal Audit.

Our role at the heart of most formal mandates is to help the business thrive. We normally don't say it so nicely; typically, we word our charters and mandates to refer to the independent, objective evaluation of key financial and operational risks, to safeguard assets, and prevent fraud. As a community of professionals, we like formality and iron-clad wording. As a function, we often fill some hallowed space in most organizations, given our reporting line directly to the Chair of the Audit Committee, the Board Chairperson, or the Chief Executive Officer.

Too often, we witness fellow Internal Auditors overplaying their independence hand. We may see this when colleagues dig in and hold their ground, their words, their opinions, and perhaps their inflexibility. Healthy challenges from management, in my experience, are generally not a bad thing if they are well-intentioned, and it is always worth listening to feedback. We need to reconcile our structured, more conservative view of risks and controls with a different, more commercial view from management. Our objectivity is as critical as our integrity, and as Internal Auditors we should always engage openly and look for practical solutions to problems.

There should be plenty of room for challenge from management, but we should always keep to the facts, the exceptions noted from sampling or data outliers that do not conform to the expected data hypothesis. From a risk culture perspective, it is important to make it clear when a line in the sand is being approached or possibly crossed by management. Cooler and calmer heads must prevail, and it should always be clear and supported by the C-Suite executives in the organization that Internal Audit must make the final call on issues and report wording and ratings.

Oftentimes, management feedback has been helpful in getting to the core issue and weakness and in helping to shape the optimal solution to the problem. We should always engage and keep an open mind. We may not always be 100-percent right, and being humble and listening is the right course of action.

If helping the business thrive is our purpose, then our distinct lens as auditors becomes one of our greatest strengths.

Internal Auditors tend to look at the world a bit differently than everyone else. Call us skeptics, but we like to verify evidence, triangulate conversations, and validate our hunches. Our lens is a few degrees to the left or right of management's lens. That is not a bad thing at all in my experience; indeed, it is often a key source of our value proposition.

In my career, working with so many talented Internal Auditors, I am constantly amazed at what Internal Auditors pick up on at the coalface when performing their fieldwork. Like funnels for knowledge, we gather a lot of assurance raw material at the top to produce a steady flow of value at the other end. Value can always be gleaned from an objective and independent viewpoint, and Internal Auditors actively look to fill that role in their organizations.

Our true value is in the eyes of our Audit Committee, Board stakeholders, and management, not necessarily our own eyes. Sometimes what we feel is valuable is not considered so by our stakeholders, and vice versa. It is important for Internal Audit leaders to be sensitive to their perceived and actual value to the organization. None of us is paid by the audit comment or report rating stratification, thankfully, but our value and worth to our organizations should remain a constant focus.

Helping the business thrive is a wonderful way to phrase Internal Audit's strategic intent. We should want management to be aware of, manage, and monitor key risks effectively. Further, we want management to have controls that support informed risk management and good outcomes, prevent fraud, and support regulatory compliance. Investing time and effort in relationship management is a critical endeavor for Internal Auditors.

As we will explore in greater detail in Chapter 14, Internal Auditors must strive to be much more than transactional counterparties; we must be adept in the art of relationship and strategic sales.

Within the organizational construct, Internal Audit is the ultimate feedback loop mechanism. Our objectivity, attention to detail, use of data analytics, and critical thinking can help the business progress. We found that some of the best perspectives we could offer came from taking a broader view of risks or standards across the organization, rather than focusing on a specific unit. Inevitably, when Internal Audit performs thematic reviews like this, we will see some areas perform well while others are plagued with exceptions or anomalies.

Providing the right perspective and context for our work is important to ensure balance and fairness. Sometimes broader, thematic audits highlight process or risk cultural issues in a specific team or function. Having a broader data set for management comparison makes it easier to grasp the points being made and can more easily spark cross-functional management conversations and benchmarking.

One topic that Internal Auditors must pay close attention to is the organization's key risks and how these risks are changing. Objective coverage and assessment of key risks is a core Internal Audit activity, but it also confirms the need for close coordination with Compliance, Risk Management, and Governance functions. Fostering harmony among the assurance functions is a worthy and necessary undertaking. We used to call ourselves the Coordinated Assurance Functions, or CAF Partners.[38] Alongside management relationship meetings, we also fostered strong relationships with our CAF colleagues, often meeting together, sharing resources, performing joint reviews periodically, and sometimes training together.

Most modern organizations have mature Internal Audit, Compliance, and Operational Risk Management functions. These functions are supported by clear mandates, and we generally coexist well together. But as a collective set of assurance providers, are we effective? Are these teams sufficiently coordinated to generate value while avoiding unnecessary overlap or conflict? Does management and the board understand the different types of assurance that each team provides?

There is a strong case for implementing a Coordinated Assurance Framework to help align assurance functions, increase risk awareness, and enhance responsiveness to create organizational value.

Within any organization, a sense of harmony, especially among the assurance functions, is a good thing. By harmony, we mean a sense of each function knowing the big picture of what the other teams are focused on, open and regular dialogue among the teams, and shared assurance objectives and risk understanding. Business stakeholders will derive value from meeting with the assurance functions together as a unit rather than having separate relationship calls.

---

38 Institute of Internal Auditors. *The IIA's Three Lines Model: An Update of the Three Lines of Defense.* Lake Mary, FL: The Institute of Internal Auditors, 2020.

Camaraderie, rather than competition, among the assurance functions is a healthier operating model. In our case, it required up-front support from the Board and Global Function Heads and helped our organization cover risks more effectively. Conversely, within an organization, there is nothing more destructive to the culture than infighting and one-upmanship occurring within the assurance functions. Partners need to act like partners.

While each team, Governance, Operational Risk Management, Compliance, and Internal Audit, had different mandates and roles, we worked well together to share perspectives and learnings, swap resources periodically, and have our voices heard and peer-challenged. Uniquely, Internal Audit provides objective and independent internal control design and operational effectiveness testing backed by samples or, in our case, full data hypotheses and analysis.

As we often referred to it, this was Assurance with a capital A. Professional guidance and assurance provided by the other CAF Partners in our organization were equally valuable and performed by very capable people who were objective but, by design, aligned more directly with the business organization. Combining these assurance capabilities and perspectives in the right mix and at the right time helps support a well-controlled organization and a strong risk culture.

Practical Steps to Help You Implement a Coordinated Assurance Framework in Your Organization

Here are six practical steps to implement a Coordinated Assurance Framework within your organization. Operating as

Coordinated Assurance Partners requires an open risk culture, a positive mindset, and a willingness to operate and share perspectives openly across department lines.

Critically, this requires the executive leaders within these functions to be catalysts, thriving on open engagement and partnership to deliver value beyond their own specific mandates. I make this point because, at the outset, having the right types of assurance leaders setting the tone from the top is a critical success factor.[39]

Step 1: Meet regularly to share perspectives among your CAF colleagues

These should be informal calls or meetings with no set agenda other than to catch up, brief each other, share perspectives, reflect on audit or other risk review work, and share operational events or regulatory developments. These meetings help to develop a shared sense of purpose and build trust among the assurance teams. Rotating who chairs the call can also help build accountability across teams.

Step 2: Strive to meet with key business stakeholders together

We met our key stakeholders at least quarterly and had a shared meeting agenda (typically one or two PowerPoint slides) and normally one representative from each assurance team. Delivering a more integrated view of assurance activities consistently adds value. Our meetings were about two-thirds

39 Committee of Sponsoring Organizations of the Treadway Commission (COSO). *Internal Control—Integrated Framework*. Durham, NC: COSO, 2013.

updates on organizational changes, key and emerging risks, business performance, and the regulatory environment, and one-third updates to the business from the CAF partners on relevant activities, outcomes, and plans within our respective functions. In these meetings, we spent the first two-thirds listening, but by sharing perspectives on assurance topics and quarterly insights, we built trust and demonstrated that we cared about the business beyond the formal audit cycle.

Step 3: Challenge key risks and emerging risks together

Shared perspectives on risks and risk impact help shape the right assurance work. We used to hold a session like this annually, with some follow-up check-ins later in the year. In our CAF calls mentioned in Step 2 above, we also referenced and discussed any big changes in the key risk matrix, which supported each assurance function in maintaining a grounded view of the business risk environment.

This also helped develop a shared view of the key risks and inherent risk levels. Internal Audit ultimately held its own risk assessment and audit planning pen and could always document a different residual risk view if necessary. However, 95-percent of the time, our starting point for audits was the organizational key risk assessments documented by our CAF partners in Risk Management and Compliance. Ongoing partnership, open dialogue, challenge, and active coordination among assurance functions will also be seen as a positive development by regulators.[40]

---

40 Financial Conduct Authority. *FG21/5: The FCA's Approach to Supervision of Internal Audit and Assurance Functions.* London: Financial Conduct Authority, 2021.

Step 4: Look for opportunities to perform joint audits, reviews, or projects, and periodically coordinate staff rotations or job swaps

These four-to-eight-week stints with a different team actively support skills development and broaden experience. Internal Audit is a great learning ground, given our critical thinking and use of agile and data-driven capabilities. Equally, it is very important to have talent movement across the various CAF teams and the business more broadly, and a well-supported rotation program is a great way to help talent move around the organization.

Over the years, several auditors moved into CAF functions and vice versa, which is a far better outcome for the organization than losing talented people to external opportunities. We also developed quarterly messages, organizational insights, typically five-to-six PowerPoint pages, together, highlighting relevant risk topics or standards that were broadly relevant to our stakeholders. Examples included risk and control disciplines over spreadsheets and best practices surrounding reliance on third-party assurance reports.

Step 5: Have input into each other's plan and look for opportunities to learn together

Before we implemented an agile audit methodology, we would hold planning sessions to ensure all our assurance activities were prioritized and that the timing of reviews was aligned to reduce overlap. At times, review sequencing was important to coordinate. We also strived to learn together, hosting business teach-ins across the CAF community and sharing social events to build knowledge and friendships. Once we became agile, the frequency of input from our CAF colleagues increased to at least quarterly and really helped to ensure that Internal Audit focused its efforts on key risks that mattered most in the moment.

Step 6: Develop heat maps together, mapping out assurance delivered against key risks and organizational units

Having this full assurance picture for the previous three years can be very helpful. We used to document this for one of our larger regulated businesses, and it proved to be a very useful analysis as a backdrop for our proposed assurance coverage of key risks with the Audit Committee. In fact, the regulator of this business regarded our coordinated risk and assurance mapping as best in class. While the risk view for any audit plan needs to be both current and forward-looking and cross-referenced to key risks, it is very useful to map out prior audit, risk, and compliance coverage and outcomes as a starting baseline. This analysis positioned Internal Audit to spark risk-based conversations with our key stakeholders, which is a very valuable exercise.

Recap of Key Learnings in this Chapter:

1. Internal Audit's organizational role is to make the business better, positioning it to thrive.

2. Our true value is in the eyes of our Audit Committee, Board stakeholders, and management, not necessarily our own eyes. Do you know what measures your key stakeholders truly value as it relates to Internal Audit performance?

3. Real organizational value can be unlocked by operating a Coordinated Assurance Framework that closely couples the assurance activities of Internal Audit, Risk Management, Compliance, and Governance functions.

4. Operating as Coordinated Assurance Partners requires an open risk culture, a positive mindset, and a willingness to operate and share perspectives openly across department lines. Critically, this requires leaders within these functions to be catalysts, setting the right tone from the top to deliver value beyond their own specific mandates.

5. Coordinated Assurance Partners share, challenge, and win together. Cross-functional team closeness and proximity support a more cohesive assurance model.

Chapter 9

MARKETING INTERNAL AUDIT TO ACHIEVE LEADERSHIP FROM EVERY SEAT

Internal Audit is among the best departments to work in to gain an organization-wide perspective. Sadly, we often don't market this fantastic learning opportunity effectively. We should be a conveyor belt for talent development and deployment and we should not be afraid to position this value proposition with the CEO and Board.

Many Internal Auditors are so focused on execution that they do not take ample time to reflect on the work environment within the Internal Audit department itself.

Other than the C-Suite, Internal Audit is one of the few places in most organizations where you can truly grasp the big picture of the organization and its culture. You can see how leaders lead, deals are done, businesses are structured, clients are engaged, rules and regulations followed, and how risks are managed and controlled.

Being a member of an Internal Audit team affords you a window into the inner workings of the organization, seeing its processes and technology at work, and understanding its strategy, client engagement, pricing, and financial performance through the lens of risks and controls. Relatively few people experience this unique perspective, given that Internal Audit typically accounts for only one to two percent of an organization's total headcount.[41]

Several years ago, we set out to develop a more proactive marketing and talent plan for our Internal Audit function. We took it upon ourselves to interview a cross-section of our management stakeholders to get their candid views on how we operate and how we are perceived. We wanted to gather some 'voice of the customer' feedback while also assessing how best to tell our story within the firm and externally to attract new talent.

One of our key interviews was with a board member who was always a strong proponent of Internal Audit. We asked him how he would best describe our work and what he felt were our strongest selling points. His response, which I paraphrase below, surprised us all.

"Internal Audit has a tough role. You parachute in like the special forces and quickly learn how a team or function works. Internal Audit grasps the key risks, processes, and controls and engages openly with management and their teams. Within six to eight weeks, Internal Audit often understands the risk and control environment better than management and identifies weaknesses and opportunities to improve.

"As partners, you listen well and care. We always appreciate your feedback, especially your insights, which are opportunities for us to further contemplate. Reporting the results timely and concisely, you wish us farewell and look to hit the repeat button for your next assignment as you drop into a totally different part of the business. I don't think many in management realize what a challenging role Internal Audit has, how adaptable you must be, and I admire all of you for doing it so well."

---

41 Institute of Internal Auditors (IIA). *The IIA Global Internal Audit Competency Framework*. (Lake Mary, FL: The Institute of Internal Auditors, 2020).

His feedback made us very proud; our only disappointment was that we had not recorded it for posterity, but I guess nobody is perfect. Internal Audit never sounded so good, so capable, so cool. We were all just wowed by the board member's perspective on our function and our team.

It was our normal practice to request feedback from key auditees after each audit, and our feedback form aligned well with our agile auditing approach. We asked about team engagement and connection with management, listening, delivery of value and insights, team capabilities, and so on.

We generally had a high response rate of around 90-percent most of the time. But overlaying the specific audit feedback with a broader 'voice of the client' initiative is a great activity for any Internal Audit team to undertake. Perhaps more positional and perception-based feedback is not such a bad thing, even if we need to be mindful of who is providing the feedback and their interactions with us. Internal Auditors are often their own worst enemies and sometimes, perhaps in our own backyard, we fail to see the wood for the trees.

What Are Our Sources of Differentiation, and are These Skill Sets or Capabilities Transferable and Sustainable?

Ask the most experienced Internal Auditors what skill they have harnessed the most while working in Internal Audit, and many will probably tell you writing and communication skills. After all, our core work product is a board-level report outlining areas requiring remediation and the actions planned to address the risks.

Audit Committees, Boards, and management generally want brief, clear reports they can trust as accurate. Overlaying our written reports is the critical need for us to present the salient points succinctly with conviction.

No Board or Audit Committee member wants to hear a Chief Auditor drone on for ages. They want an executive pitch that explains why it is important to fix the risk issues identified.

Internal Audit is a great place to learn how to write succinctly, and we have great tools to help us deliver on this. However, more broadly, Internal Audit should be identifying its top skills for its own marketing plans. Writing and communication are probably number one. Critical thinking and problem-solving are likely in the top five too, as might data analytics and the ability to handle full populations and large data sets.

Other top-tier skills could include being agile and responsive to risks, having integrity and ethics, applying logic, continuous learning, effective storytelling and presenting, and so on. More recently, artificial intelligence prompting logic has emerged as a valuable Internal Audit and assurance capability that we all should be investing in. But don't underestimate the value ascribed to being a great storyteller. Growing up in Ireland, our culture ascribed immense value to the "Seanchaí" or bearer of the spoken lore. Today, companies such as Amazon place immense value of storytelling ability to ensure key points and opportunities resonate.

Every Internal Audit team should develop a marketing plan to showcase its capabilities and sources of differentiated value. This process may also reveal gaps in desired capabilities needed to retain and attract talent. Such team reflections and analysis may feed into strategic initiatives to help the team realize its vision, and some investment in new skill sets may well be in the offing.

We used to think of our Audit function as a talent incubator for the broader organization. As a global function, we established a strong track record of placing Internal Auditors into the business, and equally, we had a good record of attracting business resources into Internal Audit. So how did we make it work?

One key aspect of our setup was that we budgeted for the equivalent of about two full-time equivalents per year, rotating into Internal Audit from business functions. This would reflect about fifteen to twenty guest auditor slots (typically six to eight weeks in duration) that we would accommodate in our key global locations. Guest auditors joined an audit team for several sprints and learned our approach. They were often specialist resources who added to our audit capabilities, but some were also just guesting for their own personal growth.

Each guest auditor would agree to an informal 'contract' up front (a one-page, self-composed commitment outlining what they hoped to gain from the experience and what they might give back to Internal Audit in the process). This program was extremely successful because we administered it directly. Our guest auditor program generally did not require Human Resources involvement or budget transfers to make it happen, given that the rotations were typically two months or less and often in the same office location.

Being a guest with Internal Audit did perhaps have a steep learning curve, but almost everyone gave positive feedback on their experiences. Our electronic workpaper system was often the biggest immediate challenge, but guests came away with an agile experience, respect for how we gathered data, developed data hypotheses, assessed outliers and outcomes, and a sense of being part of a tight-knit global team.

Some guest auditors later applied for open positions in Internal Audit and went on to become stars in our organization. All appreciated the opportunity, and their managers did too. Internal Audit also benefited from having a stable of business ambassadors who had spent time guesting with us and were more risk- and control-focused when they returned to their home teams.

Our guest auditor program was a true partnership experience and well worth the administrative effort. I think it would be great to see a change in C-Suite thinking whereby spending time in Internal Audit would be viewed as a critical experience for up-and-coming executives. Famously, some companies like General Electric have this culture,[42] but relatively few others do. That is not to say Internal Audit is not appreciated, but it is up to us to market our learning paths better within our organizations so that we have more of a line outside our door.

In a similar way, Internal Audit staff would request rotations into various business functions. Sometimes this was to develop relationships given career ambitions; other times it was for personal growth and the development of new technical skills. Having strong C-Suite and Managing Director relationships helped Internal Audit open doors for our talent.

There was good reciprocity from our business partners, and these short-term rotations, typically eight weeks or so, served us well. For me, a key benefit was enabling Internal Auditors who had only worked in Internal Audit to experience business life on the other side of the fence, as I did mid-career when I worked in Projects, Strategy, and Fixed Income Coverage roles. There is always value in experiencing life through a different lens, and these rotations helped talent mobility and infused more commercial DNA within our team. We always felt it was much better for our organization that talented people move internally rather than lose them externally, given the continuous investment and development of our people.

Most Internal Audit departments offer a lifelong continuous learning journey, but it is up to each person to take advantage of the opportunity. As a team and as individuals, we used to set forth our existing top skills and those new skills we wanted to

42 Tichy, Noel M., and Stratford Sherman. *Control Your Destiny or Someone Else Will: How Jack Welch Is Making General Electric the World's Most Competitive Company.* New York: Doubleday, 1993.

develop in the coming 12 to 18 months. This is a wonderful exercise to perform, and you can have a page for technical skills and another for soft or power skills. Those who had mastered specific skills could coach others looking to develop them. New skills desired would prompt discussion on the best paths to develop those skills (rotations, job swaps, specific audits, certifications, training courses, and so on).

We encouraged informal teach-ins on specific skill topics in-house. We would put them in the calendar, bring our lunches, and be there. Fostering new skill sets also had additional benefits; team members would gain coaching and presentation experience with a friendly audience. As a Chief Audit Executive, one step I really liked discussing with more junior members of the team was the pursuit of new certifications.

We always found the budget to pay for these programs and courses. Indeed, many years later as I reflect, witnessing teammates successfully completing certifications is one of the most rewarding experiences as a leader. Seeing those letters after their names and knowing that we had those early discussions and coaching sessions to encourage them a few years earlier makes me proud.

Unfortunately, effective marketing is probably not near the top of Internal Audit's collective skill sets. So how should we go about marketing Internal Audit for success? We spent time developing a marketing plan several years ago. We loved the tagline 'Come in, We're Open for Business'. Our focus was marketing who we are, what we do, and how and why we do it. Just describing our core capabilities, transferable skill sets, and learning opportunities in a 10–12-page slide deck was a great shared learning exercise.

These materials really helped us tell our story. How many of you, as accountants and auditors, have mentioned your job at a party only to have someone assume you must be busy submitting tax returns? I have heard that so many times, and while I take pride in completing my own taxes, that is about the sum of my tax experience. This well-worn example highlights a key point; our perception by others matters, which is why it is so important for us to set the record straight. Developing and sharing an effective marketing plan is key to success in this regard.

We shared our marketing plan with our key relationship stakeholders in the business to get the word out. It was tangible, had links to our intranet page, key offerings, and useful contacts. Many of the slides were used when we met with our regulators to help set the stage, updating them on our footprint and key selling points.

We shared the slides with staff looking to be guest auditors and with internal candidates interviewing for positions in Internal Audit. We outlined our mandate and charter, but more than that, we outlined the opportunities to develop transferable skills and capabilities working in Internal Audit, particularly data analysis, critical thinking, and executive communication. We also outlined how we as a team were catalysts for positive change in our organization through relationships, quarterly messages, insights, and our more formal reports.

Key headings we used within our marketing plan slides, included:

- Organization and leadership
- High-level charter and risk coverage mandate
- Global footprint
- Diversity of people, qualifications, and experience levels
- Our vision, our journey, and our risk culture
- Opportunities to develop transferable and differentiating skill sets and to embrace continuous learning
- How we partner with the business teams and our talent movement successes
- Product offering
- Key contacts

Developing marketing materials for Internal Audit really helped me as a Chief Audit Executive. Marketing the function and team is one set of critical endeavors, but leading the team effectively is another. Internal Audit leaders (Managers, Directors, and Chief Audit Executives) routinely face many challenges balancing the pressure of delivering impact and value to stakeholders and management while also leading the team, setting a high professional bar, ensuring a team-oriented work environment that supports quality work, and fostering a risk-based culture.

In my experience, the most effective Internal Audit leaders have a lot of empathy for their team members. After all, we were all Staff Auditors, or on the bottom rung of the ladder ourselves, at some point. Empathy and humility are great audit leadership superpowers to develop. Listening to team members' input and purposely giving up the mic to others to let them speak are also great leadership behaviors.

As the adage goes, a problem shared is a problem halved. That is how we used to operate in my team. We had an open, flat team structure. We practiced agile auditing, so while I was the product owner, I sat in on daily calls mostly in listening mode (listening to facts and updates, but also to team asks for help, promoting team discussion and learning, and helping with any key stakeholders).

Our team meetings always started with an open mic session for shared learnings. We encouraged team members to share nuggets of value, approaches to challenges that worked, useful resources and tools, and so on. Not surprisingly, our team motto was, 'We succeed together, and we fail together.' Yes, you could say it was very 'Three Musketeerish,' but it kept us together as a team. Indeed, even after I moved companies, many in my former team remain good friends, both in the Americas and Europe. We lived these values, and being an agile audit team helped us.

As a leader, we had open conversations at all levels in the team (from intern to the Directors reporting directly to me). Harmony is powerful in a team; you can truly sense when everyone is rowing in the same direction. Having diverse teams is also a strong point. We were lucky to have many different backgrounds, cultures, and skills in our team, and our overall work product was better for it.

Developing and delivering an effective Internal Audit marketing strategy is a must-do activity for all Internal Audit leaders. Below, I outline some of the more impactful leadership traits that can make a real difference in how you are perceived and valued as a leader within Internal Audit. Focusing on how these traits and related activities are positioned and marketed to management is a critical success factor.

Audit Leadership Trait Number One – Having Executive Pitch and Being Credible in Describing Control Points in Risk Terms

Sometimes as a Chief Audit Executive, agreeing to disagree is the outcome that is needed. There is no need to be personal, just open, honest, and candid. I recall presenting to the Audit Committee an unsatisfactory audit report where management did not agree with the final audit rating, which in our organization was an extremely rare occurrence. It had been quite a testy audit report closing process in the weeks before the Audit Committee meeting.

During my update, I reflected on the results and noted that Internal Audit was comfortable that management had developed appropriate action plans to remediate the issues and risks raised. We noted that management did not agree with the final rating assigned to the audit report, but in the end, that was our role as an objective function. It was not personal, and despite the difference in opinion, management was taking the right steps to remediate the issues. While it was a regional Audit Committee, the Group's Chief Risk Officer sat in on the meeting on this occasion.

Later that evening, at a drinks reception immediately before the Board dinner, he took me aside and told me that he was really impressed with how I pitched the difference of opinion and found the poise to balance the argument while keeping it all factual. The function in question was part of his global organization, and he accepted that the rating of Internal Audit reports was our role, not management's. Indeed, we later learned that he brought the topic up with his own direct reports and made his views on the matter clear. Phew, I thought he was coming over to take me to the woodshed!

Another example from earlier in my career was when we delivered a report from a special investigation to the CEO of one of the organization's business units. Without going into details, it was a transaction that had gone horribly wrong over several years, and our organization had lost a fortune.

You can understand how the Audit Committee Chair was very keen to support an independent investigation of the matter, and we were given that special mandate. Over about a month, we interviewed all the executives involved and candidly got their perspectives, reviewed the transaction documentation, and generated a diary of events in chronological order (who knew what and when).

The CEO in question read the report over a weekend, and my boss and I were summoned to the CEO's office early the next week to discuss it. The CEO opened the meeting as follows, and I paraphrase: *"I read your report over the weekend; in fact, I read it twice. I thought I understood that transaction so well when it all went south a couple of months back, but reading your report, I learned so much more about the transaction that I did not understand fully or perceive clearly when it was explained to me. Well done, this is an excellent report."* Phew, again.

Joking aside, we had integrity and objectivity and wanted to present an accurate report of what had happened so lessons could be learned and failures not repeated. Being credible and objective helped us connect with the CEO.

After that investigation, our relationship was stronger and more open, as he had gained respect for our capabilities and trusted us more. Interestingly, the following year, when we held our annual planning session with management (this was a few decades ago, to be clear), the CEO attended in person too. It was a bit strange for people to see the CEO and his key divisional executives camping out in the large Internal Audit conference room instead of the boardroom. A small gesture, you might say, but it was evidence of trust in us as a team and of setting the right tone from the top.

Audit Leadership Trait Number Two – Expressing Forward-Looking Risk Views in Practical Ways and Delivering the Right Type of Audit at the Right Time

Great Internal Audit leaders anticipate risks and are always scanning the horizon for outsized risks that could harm the organization. Even when all our 'Spidey senses' are alert and working, we still need to develop credible proposals. When risks are moving quickly and circumstances are changing, it may be better to demonstrate product agility and suggest a nimbler review, with a targeted scope and perhaps an unrated outcome.

I have always been a big proponent of rating issues so that Executive Management and the Board Audit Committee can better prioritize resources and governance choices. I have no problem issuing an unrated audit report in the right circumstances. This was often perceived as being commercial and fair. In my experience, management is typically the first to agree and support major issues coming from any audit work.

With product agility, we can also be more creative. Most Internal Audit functions employ a breadth of different products, and we should not be afraid to use them. We always tried to foresee the likely results and learnings, then asked ourselves what product would likely generate results that would be valuable and could be syndicated. We will discuss audit product agility in our next chapter, but suffice it to say, if you want to be an Internal Audit rockstar, you must be more than a one-hit wonder!

Audit Leadership Trait Number Three – Be a Great Business Sparring Partner, Demonstrate Caring, and Take Interest in Enabling Business Successes and Preventing Failures

One of the greatest compliments an Internal Audit leader can receive from management is being called a worthy sparring partner. Using the boxing analogy, title fighters rely on sparring partners to help train them for the upcoming match with their opponent. The sparring partner's role is to mimic the opponent's punching style, reach, and footwork to help the prizefighter prepare for the real fight. When the boxer wins the title match, you don't often hear about the sparring partners, but they are the unsung heroes of the day.

Challenge from Internal Audit is a good thing. Asking good questions, making management think, and seeing risks or themes that may be lurking below the surface are all behaviors that help management build resilience and become more responsive to risk.

Sparring has, by its nature, an element of back and forth. That is fine between Internal Audit and management, and we should welcome it, as it should deliver better outcomes. In an Internal Audit sense, being a sparring partner not only speaks to the challenge and assurance provided, but also to the issues and opportunities being identified. While our primary audit objective is to highlight risk and control weaknesses, our secondary role is to provide feedback, opportunities, and insights for management reflection.

In my former team, the latter were discussed and suggested as areas where management could dig a bit deeper and develop any actions they felt were worthwhile. There was no formality to it; just Internal Audit being a catalyst for positive organizational change. Now ask yourself, who wouldn't want this type of feedback from their Internal Auditors?

Audit Leadership Trait Number Four – Empower Leadership from Every Team Seat and Harmony Across the Team

Every Chief Audit Executive has a different leadership style. Some are old-school expert leaders who still seek to command and control everybody and everything that happens in their team. I am not a fan of that style at all, as it is too restrictive and supports leadership from only one seat instead of from every seat in the team. Being a servant or catalyst leader is a wonderful leadership style for Internal Audit executives.[43]

These leadership styles do not imply you are a pushover; far from it. Catalyst leaders are agile and approachable. They listen well and know how to set shared objectives, when to push, and when to pull. They seek team empowerment and actively play a coaching role, always there to pitch in when needed to help team members succeed. They want the team and the business

43 Robert K. Greenleaf, *Servant Leadership: A Journey into the Nature of Legitimate Power and Greatness* (New York: Paulist Press, 1977).

to succeed and will intercede to prevent individual or team failure. When every team member is contributing ideas and staying attentive, Internal Audit just purrs along.

Harmony is such a great trait of a team with high performance and high integrity. Everyone is contributing and caring about the big-picture outcomes. We used to ask everyone to chip in at team meetings to provide suggestions and updates from their seats (what they liked and what was on their mind). As a leader, fostering open dialogue is a great thing. Often, a team member is very relieved to raise a worry or concern, and as leaders, we need to take stock of team needs and wants, being flexible enough to rally the troops without causing undue anxiety or stress.

I used to help by setting tight turnaround times on my end to review items (issues, reports, sprint review documents, and so on) so I was not holding things up. The team really appreciated that. Shane could be relied upon to deliver feedback within 24 to 36 hours and always encouraged open team discussion of issues and reports.

Audit Leadership Trait Number Five – Actively Coach the Team and Allow Deputies to Trial and Step Up so that a Bench of Talent is Being Developed

As we discussed in Chapters 4 and 5, everybody needs a coach to succeed. Many of us learned from our managers, who took us under their wings and made the learning journey doable and fun. They provided a safe space for us to learn on the job and, at times, to fail. We learn the most in life from our failures, not our successes. As Internal Audit leaders, we must help our deputies develop and give them room to trial the next level.

We can achieve this in many ways. We always liked to bring key deputies into the process of developing Audit Committee update materials (learning how to be precise while being informative). The next step would be to have the deputy deliver the Audit Committee update and be involved in the pre-meetings with the Audit Committee Chair. Obviously, we cleared this with the Chair, explaining our rationale for building the talent bench, which was an interest they shared.

When you show your team members you care about them and want them to be ready when it is their time to step up, they will really appreciate it. My deputies were all wonderful auditors. They were smart, passionate about their jobs, and willing to go above and beyond without being asked. That is a great place to be as a Chief Audit Executive, knowing that you have executive talent developing.

In Audit Committee meetings, initially I would be there, always willing to chime in or answer any tough questions. I had their backs if needed. Sometimes things did not quite go as planned; we would lick our wounds and take on the feedback. We celebrated our shared successes and were open, honest, and candid about our failures. We strived never to make the same mistake twice.

Audit Leadership Trait Number Six – Set an Aspirational Vision for the Internal Audit Team, Deliver It and Live It

To be a leader, you must have a vision (not just anticipating the future path of the team, but actively setting a high bar, a North Star, to help instill a culture of continuous improvement and learning within your team). For Internal Audit, this is not an easy leadership responsibility, given that the team spends most of its time in audit execution or reporting mode.

Great Internal Audit leaders develop and syndicate a shared vision with their teams and secure strong buy-in to deliver it. For me, as a Chief Audit Executive, one of the most rewarding parts of my role within our global Internal Audit Executive team was helping to set our vision and then syndicating and delivering it over a multiyear journey.

This requires constant assessment and reprioritization, and if you are not devoting substantial time to realizing your team's vision, you are failing in terms of ambition and inspiration. Talented Internal Auditors are always learning new skills and applying technology, so this is among the most critical Internal Audit leadership responsibilities.

Marketing Maestros of the Rock and Roll World

In the world of rock music, one band stands alone in my eyes as the greatest marketers of all time: Kiss.[44] Yes, Gene Simmons, Paul Stanley, Ace Frehley, and Peter Criss, between them, perfected the art of marketing themselves, their music, and their personas to their fans. With their heavy makeup, platform boots, and distinct on-stage personas, Kiss is certainly a unique band. From humble beginnings in Queens, New York, they rose to become one of the biggest rock acts globally for many decades.

Most of their hits were in the mid to late seventies and eighties, so you might wonder how Kiss remained so big. In their

44 David Leaf and Ken Sharp, *KISS: Behind the Mask—The Official Authorized Biography* (New York: Warner Books, 2003).

50th year, they sold out large arenas across the globe night after night. As a band, Kiss mastered their branding and merchandising like no other.

Kiss sold more than their music. They sold belief. Internal Audit must do the same. Our 'fans' are our stakeholders, and their loyalty is earned through clarity, consistency, and confidence.

Long after their music faded from its peak, their branding and marketing kept them relevant. The Kiss Army, as their fan base is known, has legions of followers all over the world. Known for big, spectacular shows, high energy, and theatrics, Kiss remains one of the most successful rock bands to this day. They have even created digital versions of themselves as full retirement perhaps beckons.

They are masters of the client experience, supporting their brand ruthlessly to attract newer, younger fans. Driven to succeed, the Kiss Army has spawned new generations of young fans wanting to emulate their favorite character.

So, what can Internal Auditors learn from Kiss?

The most obvious lesson is the power of marketing to support our brand and to keep us relevant. Kiss never got complacent. They put their image on a wide variety of products and services that appealed to their fan base. They kept investing in their brand and, importantly, changing with the times and technology.

Internal Auditors must also invest consistently in our brand, proactively marketing our services and impact. Like Kiss, we should not be afraid to flex our product set to satisfy our stakeholders and adopt new technology. If Internal Auditors want to remain relevant, we must have a modern proposition supported by clear branding and marketing impact. Like Kiss, Internal Auditors must not be afraid to define a new path to value and relevance within their organizations.

Recap of Key Learnings in this Chapter:

1. Make time to develop a marketing plan for your Internal Audit function. Stopping and pausing to assess your sources of sustainable value and key selling points to attract talent will be time well spent.

2. Share the story of Internal Audit's journey and impact with your Audit Committee, Board, and management stakeholders, and position your function as a talent incubator for your organization.

3. Strive to be a great sparring partner for the business. Show that you care about the business and make time for informal conversations.

4. Set a clear, aspirational vision for your Internal Audit team.

Recap of Key Learnings in this Chapter:

5. Be catalysts for positive change in your organization. Coach your team actively, let deputies step up in safe ways, and live shared team values.

6. Marketing your Internal Audit capabilities is not a one-and-done exercise. It requires ongoing attention and refreshment to keep your message up to date and relevant to your stakeholders. Love them or hate them, you must give Kiss their due for their marketing creativity, and endurance.

Chapter 10

LEVERAGING PRODUCT AGILITY, DATA ANALYTICS TO DELIVER FORWARD-LOOKING ASSURANCE

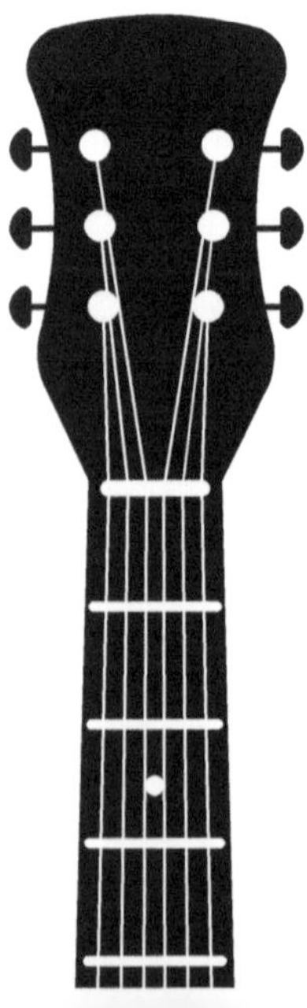

The world of Internal Audit continues to change and evolve daily. Big data, digitalization, and Artificial Intelligence are transforming businesses while simultaneously increasing stakeholders' expectations of Internal Audit teams globally.

All Internal Audit teams that I know want to be relevant and help shape the corporate persona of their organizations. We want to provide valued, independent feedback and insights, helping the business to be more successful in managing risks while achieving great outcomes for our organizations, clients, and people. We can deploy any number of audit products to help us deliver this value if we are creative and open to taking on the challenge.

Now is the time to have a range of audit products available to meet increased stakeholder demand, and we should strive to be much more than a single scoop of plain vanilla ice cream. Variety is the spice of life, as the old saying goes, and these words ring true for Internal Audit teams looking to use different audit products to deliver value.

Many Internal Audit teams have developed a product suite to better enable risk coverage within their organizations: an audit product continuum. This is particularly true in progressive and agile audit teams. Having a viable audit product catalogue requires Internal Audit to be flexible, stay close to business leaders and the operating risk environment, and, dare I say it, be less perfectionist.

Risk and risk scenarios come in all forms, complexities, and sizes. Audit products need to follow suit. Internal Auditors need the confidence and gravitas to adapt their products to fit the types of risks being reviewed. The end needs to justify the means, and nothing frustrates management more than Internal Audit demonstrating it is a one-hit wonder.

Being creative, open, and agile will help your Audit Team have the courage to challenge the existing audit product status quo. While there is no perfect answer as to which products to have in your tool bag, here is an indicative outline of audit products that I have seen over the years that have worked. Internal Audit teams should be looking for audit products that support value delivery, identifying issues and insights relative to risks that matter to the organization.

My broad recommendation is for Internal Audit teams to be progressive and to make use of some shorter-duration products to unlock value more quickly where possible. Many of us have experienced value- and reputation-destroying audits, for example, a 90-day audit with no issues, a global audit that fails to cover the biggest business segment, or an audit that occurs a year after the risk scenario being contemplated has already been crystallized. In audit product terms, we must have different horses for different courses, driven by flexibility and commerciality.

Some Common Types of Audit Products

- Full Data Audit: Typically covers end-to-end processes and involves multiple systems or data repositories. These are large, complex audits that use data science and data hypotheses to test the completeness and outcomes of full populations. Typically lasts six to seven two-week sprints, especially if covering a global scope.

- Data-Driven Audit: Usually focused on a specific data lake or repository; uses data hypotheses to test full population completeness and outcomes, processing policies, standards, and regulations. Typically lasts three to four two-week sprints.
- Traditional Audit Using Sample-Based Testing: A well-established practice in our profession, though if not agile, these audits can over-audit low-level risks if not time-boxed.
- Management's Risk and Controls Self-Assessment Audit: These can be very enlightening audits to assess whether management is open, honest, and candid by validating how management concludes on their risk and controls and by reviewing the supporting evidence. These reviews should be smaller than a typical audit, and they can also help validate the quality and rigor of the organization's Enterprise Risk Management and Risk Control Self-Assessment practices. Typically lasts two to three two-week sprints.
- Forward-Looking Project or Transformation Audit: These audits usually require a subject-matter expert in the area being reviewed. They are more of a candid, independent risk assessment of the project at a point in time and require a thorough understanding of the transformation plan, timeframes, and risk scenarios.
- Systems Delivery Audits: Pre-implementation or post-implementation reviews are well-established practices. Pre-implementation reviews focus on the adequacy of control design; post-implementation reviews may focus on control design and initial operational effectiveness, helping management work out the kinks as early as possible.

- Consulting or Advisory Review: Often focused on risk understanding and the effectiveness of control design and initial implementation. These are great in terms of Line 1 and Line 2 partnering, but they can also drain resources if not adequately time boxed.
- Targeted Audit: Typically, a limited-scope audit with one or two objectives. Results tend to be binary, meaning they are either good or not good. Usually small in effort, involving one to two two-week sprints.

Having a range of audit products with different shapes and sizes is a good thing. Internal Audit can flex its style and adapt its coverage more quickly, and management and the Audit Committee would presumably support audit products that cut to the chase. Each of the above types of audit products is valuable.

However, one area where Internal Audit may have more room to grow is in performing rapid risk and control improvement reviews. In most organizations, despite modern systems, digitalization, and the use of data analysis and artificial intelligence, Internal Audits still take several months to complete.

Many years ago, we used to have a saying in our department: you can't rush an audit, it needs a start, a middle, and an end. Back then, we had a 90-day rule, and even then, many audits, especially global ones, took four, five, or even six months to get out the door. Performing large, global audits with broad scopes didn't help our cause, to be blunt.

While that perspective may smell of old-world, traditional auditing, I do think that many Internal Audit teams today are much nimbler and use agile methodologies to guide the deployment of resources to key risks. However, is there a case for a much shorter, intense, and collaborative audit product with management? Internal Audits routinely take 60 to 90 days to complete, even those performed using agile audit methodologies.

Call me an old-fashioned auditor, but back when I was an Audit Senior and Audit Manager working in a Wall Street investment bank, most of my audit points were identified initially through management discussion. I was always in listening mode, trying to understand cases that were outliers and exceptions. Management's input was a useful guide, and it typically helped me hone my judgmental samples for testing.

We would support any points being raised with examples from the testing to ensure our observations were valid, but in many cases, it was management interaction that was key to identifying outsized or unexpected risks or transactions. Rolling that logic forward a few decades, Internal Audit and Coordinated Assurance Partners like Compliance, Risk Management, and Governance teams should be hosting rapid improvement risk and control sessions with management to help the organization progress. Let's call these sessions Management Audit Challenge Sessions, or MACS for short.

The Case for Rapid Risk and Control Management Audit Challenge Sessions

As our audit cycles shorten, it is imperative that we roll up our sleeves and engage more directly with management on risks and controls. Years ago, our global Internal Audit Executive Leadership team used to have cube sessions with one of the Big 4 firms in London. These involved expert Internal Audit practitioners and our global Executive Management team reviewing emerging risks and topics in a glass conference room (cube).

These were great learning and reflection sessions, and we always came away with a few nuggets in terms of takeaways and strategic actions. These sessions took hours, not weeks or months.

Internal Audit should be looking to deliver similar value in short, rapid bursts as part of its overall product repertoire.

If we held a challenge session for three or four hours and identified an issue or two with solutions, wouldn't that be a fantastic outcome and return on investment for half a day's work? Of course, it would. Good things can come in small packages!

Many of us have either heard this or said it ourselves; the holiday gift of jewelry is often the source, I suspect. Now, in the world of Internal Audit products, we have a continuum of audit types and services to offer. Perhaps our collective challenge is to get comfortable with the uncomfortable feeling that less sometimes translates into more, a lot more.

In rock music, one analogy could be the length of a song, from Lynyrd Skynyrd's Freebird[45] (nine minutes of the perfect southern rock song) to The Ramones' Blitzkrieg Bop[46] (just over two minutes of fast, intense punk) and everything in between.

Rock Music's 'Big Three': Steve Marriott, Ronnie James Dio, and Klaus Meine

These rock singers[47] are widely regarded as having some of the biggest and best voices in rock music, strong and operatic, with amazing range. It is sometimes hard to believe, given that one other trait they shared was their diminutive size. Ranging

45 Lynyrd Skynyrd, *Freebird*, recorded 1973, on *Pronounced 'Lĕh-'nérd 'Skin-'nérd*, MCA Records, 1973.

46 The Ramones, *Blitzkrieg Bop*, recorded 1976, on *Ramones*, Sire Records, 1976.

47 Rolling Stone. "The 100 Greatest Singers of All Time." *Rolling Stone*, updated January 2023. https://www.rollingstone.com/music/music-lists/100-greatest-singers-of-all-time-147019/

between 5'2" and 5'4", none of them fit the bill as intimidating rock and roll frontmen. Many made that mistake until they heard them belt out a few tunes. Humble Pie's Thirty Days in the Hole,[48] Black Sabbath's (with Ronnie James Dio) Neon Knights,[49] or The Scorpions' Rock You Like a Hurricane[50] is all I need to say.

The lesson for Internal Auditors is that less is often more, whether in the simplicity of a song (in terms of the notes not played as much as the notes played) or in the power and range that can come from singers like Steve, Ronnie, or Klaus, who do not check the normal boxes. So, don't be afraid to experiment with smaller, more targeted assurance products and less formal types of reviews. Great things can indeed come from small packages.

At times, I feel that Internal Audit teams take too much pride in the structured component of their work, and while this structure (whether sprints or traditional audit planning, fieldwork testing, and reporting phases) is valuable, it can impede Internal Audit's timeliness and relevance.

In our digital world, there are growing stakeholder expectations for Internal Audit to deliver real value more quickly. Holding some rapid risk and control Management/Audit Challenge Sessions could be particularly useful for key risks (to gauge if a full audit should be considered) or to provide right-sized assurance on moderate-risk areas a bit lower down the totem pole.

Internal Audit teams should be looking to strategically use their full product suite to have more impact here and now. Periodically deploying focused, shorter-duration audit products should enable faster value delivery on specific risk topics.

---

48 Humble Pie, *Thirty Days in the Hole,* recorded 1972, on *Smokin',* A&M Records, 1972.

49 Black Sabbath, *Neon Knights,* recorded 1980, on *Heaven and Hell,* Vertigo Records, 1980.

50 Scorpions, *Rock You Like a Hurricane,* recorded 1984, on *Love at First Sting,* Harvest/EMI Records, 1984.

In a similar vein, Internal Audit should be looking to perform and revise data hypothesis testing over full populations with management, and much more in real time. At a former employer, we had the capability in our audit team to flex data hypotheses in real time; this was the normal ebb and flow of Audit team sessions with our data scientists.

For example, sometimes we would run a hypothesis but use the wrong field. Once we identified the right field, our data scientists would rerun the hypotheses and show us the revised results in real time. The only people missing were management. We conducted these sessions virtually during the global pandemic, which may well be indicative of how we should approach data-driven audits in the future.

It does not take too much imagination to see an Internal Audit of the future being a more real-time validation of data hypotheses and outcomes directly with management. Food for thought. Throw in AI, and we are not too far away from that reality.

Another key consideration in developing a broader audit product offering is our ability to deliver more forward-looking assurance. Trailing organizational activity by six to eighteen months and relying on sample testing is akin to taking a driving lesson while only looking in the rearview mirror. The road ahead is in front of us, and it is time to change our audit perspective. So, what now?

C-Suite executives want near real-time risk and control feedback, and they value forward-looking views on the organization's business activities and data or infrastructure models, risks that are at or just over the horizon. Collectively, this may represent a polar shift for Internal Audit teams, as it requires much more forward-looking assessments, the use of full data and data hypotheses, shorter audit cycles, and greater focus on organizational transformation risks.

Identifying and preventing potential issues will become as integral as reporting on and remediating problems that have already happened. The audit of the future may comprise auditors and management reviewing data sets and hypotheses together, virtually or in a conference room, adapting hypotheses in real time to review data conformance and outcomes. That is not far away, and some Audit teams that have invested early in data science skills are already well along this path. The audit cycles of the future will be measured in days and weeks, not months, and the deployment of predictive analytics and powerful Artificial Intelligence tools will increase the pace of change and Internal Audit adoption.

Transformation risk is a critical area for Internal Audit focus. How many large projects remain in green status up until a few months before the intended go-live date, only to move swiftly to red status and stay there, often going well past the original target delivery date as reality hits? This scenario happens almost all the time in nearly every organization, unfortunately, particularly when using the waterfall project management approach.

Agile methodology may help, given its focus on tackling the most valuable tasks first (often the most difficult components upfront).[51] Even when projects go live or new systems are migrated into production, it is not unusual for a large Day 2 book of work to remain, reflecting the functionality that didn't work effectively or did not pass component, end-to-end, or user acceptance testing.

So where is Internal Audit? Internal Audit needs to devote its resources to auditing risks and topics that matter, here and now. Internal Audit should strive to review large change programs actively, including health checks early on to assess and challenge management's risk awareness. In this sense, an audit health check review must be forward-looking, and Audit will need subject matter expertise to be credible and add real value.

51 Beck, Kent et al. *Manifesto for Agile Software Development*. Agile Alliance, 2001. https://agilemanifesto.org/.

Such reviews should be welcomed by management, as working with Audit to assess where the planned transformation stands (in terms of requirements definition, dependency clarity, cross-functional working culture, resourcing, and reporting transparency) demonstrates a positive risk culture. Equally, issues identified early will better position the organization for successful delivery.

Internal Audit should also be performing full-data audits, providing full-population assurance over the last 12 to 18 months of data right up to the start date of the audit. Using data hypotheses to define the expected truths in the data set, Audit should be able to size true exceptions fully and increase the breadth of assurance dramatically.

Full-data audits demonstrate great transparency and support richer insights. Among Internal Audit's key strengths are critical thinking and the ability to review data and outcomes in a structured way. Oftentimes, the discipline of running (and sometimes adapting and re-running) data hypotheses will provide Internal Audit with useful areas and topics to feed back to management. There is always value in having an independent view, especially on large datasets.

Auditors tend to pick up on things quickly; they are always looking for non-conformance and tend to be excellent at making or implying observations as they assess risks, controls, processes, evidence, and the handling of non-standard items. Insights may not be internal control weaknesses today, but they can represent forward-looking opportunities for management.

Audit should provide feedback on these insights actively, in effect, offering feedback on risk culture, data monitoring, data patterns, and best practices that were identified during the audit. These should be framed as opportunities for management to assess and possibly investigate further if they feel warranted. In this way, sharing insights can position Internal Audit as a catalyst function that supports positive risk culture change within the organization.

Recap of Key Learnings in this Chapter:

1. Product agility and having a range of audit products to deploy is a must-have for the modern, agile Internal Audit department.

2. Invest time to develop and host rapid risk and control improvement sessions with Coordinated Assurance Partners and management. Look to cover more risks across your total risk universe in short, smart bursts through these rapid risk and control assessment sessions and use them to add value quickly while building trust. Such short, sharp risk reviews can support better Internal Audit risk coverage, including quick assessments of areas not perceived to be risky but which might highlight areas worthy of a more detailed audit.

3. Forward-looking assurance is a growing stakeholder expectation of Internal Audit.

4. C-Suite executives want near real-time risk and control feedback, and they value forward-looking views on the organization's business activities and data or infrastructure models, risks that are at or just over the horizon.

Recap of Key Learnings in this Chapter:

5. Use data hypotheses to perform full-data audits. Reviewing full data populations provides management and the board with far greater assurance and enables Internal Audit to size issues more accurately. It's a win-win strategy.

6. Less is often more: more valuable, succinct, and appreciated. When it comes to our Internal Audit Product catalogue, we should be inspired by the musical range and depth offered by Steve Marriott, Ronnie James Dio, and Klaus Meine.

Chapter 11

AUDITING CORPORATE STRATEGY AND STRATEGIC CHANGE INITIATIVES FOR IMPACT

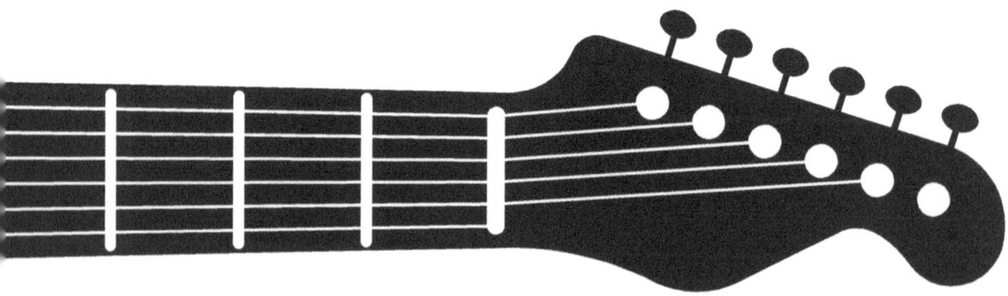

Strategy leaders project vision. Internal Audit leaders project reality. Great organizations survive only when both speak the same risk language so different views can be reconciled.

Call me a bit sarcastic, but I've always sensed that those who are best at devising great strategies and seeing big-picture opportunities that others cannot, often lack implementation skills. Few people can comfortably move from a fifty-thousand-foot perspective to a two-foot one. I've only met a couple of people like this in my career, and they are absolutely the exception to the rule.

One former internal client, an executive at a large UK insurance company, comes to mind, and perhaps noteworthy, he started his career in Internal Audit. Affirming that an organization's strategy is on track and progressing as expected is among the greatest and most important challenges in the modern organization.

All the C-Suite executives and board members are relying on many more junior officers and leaders to deliver the vision they have set forth. Providing challenge and assurance over corporate strategy is a critical area for Internal Audit, yet many teams steer clear of this topic because it requires unconventional thinking and can be politically fraught.

Who wants to tell the Chairman or CEO that the implementation of a key strategy is at risk or possibly failing outright? Will you be considered a hero or a zero? Might it be a case of shooting the messenger?

Auditing strategy is an area where you earn your stripes. You may well end up with some battle scars too, but the organization will be better off if Internal Audit provides open, honest, and candid feedback in this space.

Auditing Strategy

In most organizations, strategic change takes time, often the epitome of multi-year projects and initiatives. Lately, digitization and AI have helped to ramp up change delivery timetables.[52] Speed of delivery is increasing. It is very common for a dichotomy to exist between those senior executives setting a strategic path and those managers tasked with delivering the changes on the ground, whether along customer, product, people, process, or culture dimensions. Herein lies the source of much organizational angst: how to reconcile strategic change plans and intent with progress, acceptance, and support among employees and managers on the ground. It is the organizational intersection where the Ivy League meets Community College. Keeping these constituencies aligned is critical, and Internal Auditors must remain aware of the need for broad organizational alignment around strategy. For example, key questions that Internal Audit can help answer include:

- Does the strategic change align with the organization's overall goals and values?

52 McKinsey & Company. *The State of AI in 2024: Accelerating Change and Transformation.* New York: McKinsey Global Institute, 2024.

- Who is responsible for designing and reaffirming this alignment?
- Who reconciles the top-down view to the bottom-up view across the organization, and how is this critical step performed?
- What forums exist to enable open, honest, and candid discussions and feedback?

Deviations will likely be needed along the change journey to keep alignment with the value proposition and technology improvements and to overcome implementation challenges and obstacles. Internal Audit's review of strategy should include these questions, providing an objective perspective on whether the setup and alignment are strong, moderate, or weak.

Strategic change in an organization often requires fresh thinking and expertise that the organization may need to hire to ensure the intended strategy is credible. No matter the size or scale of the change, it is critical to set forth measures of success.

What are the key metrics, data points, and outcomes that would support success throughout the journey? It is essential for sponsors of strategic change to support their vision with reality. Just like Internal Audit assessing its own progress in delivering its vision, business management and project implementation teams must regularly make candid assessments of value delivery (or failure to deliver).

Movement away from the originally envisioned target may be required as costs, technology innovation, expected customer service differentiation, and timeframes all come into focus. We should be asking whether the change journey is being broken down into logical chunks and whether risks across each chunk are actively measured and assessed.

Internal Audit can provide objective feedback on strategic change delivery, and given the scale, complexity, and speed of delivery, this may require a small, dedicated Audit team to spend a lot of time getting into the fabric of the strategic change program.

Embedding Internal Audit resources into the strategic change program is one way to ensure knowledge transfer and focus audit resources on the risks that matter. This may be a relatively big resource investment from an Internal Audit perspective, but it is possibly justified when covering strategic risks for the organization, particularly those that are more immediate.

While every strategic change program will be different, a general roadmap for Internal Audit coverage and risk assessment is set forth below. The list is by no means exhaustive, but if applied, it should provide valuable, objective assurance on strategic changes within the organization. An important factor to consider is whether strategic change programs are unique or part of a larger, global portfolio of change.

The role of Internal Audit within a large transformation program is forward-looking; it will require more sense-checking and intuition, more candid conversations with project stakeholders, risk owners, and managers than in our normal audit work. It will require Internal Audit team members to be comfortable with being uncomfortable, as they may feel more direct challenge from project experts and perhaps feel thrown in at the deep end of the pool initially.

That said, Internal Auditors typically have strong sensory perception and will quickly pick up the project's breadcrumbs once immersed in the transformation program, understanding its strategic intent, cost benefits, and resourcing requirements, among other dimensions of change.

Program Governance

A key starting point for Internal Audit is to assess that the Program Governance Office and Program Steering Board have been established and resourced with suitably skilled professionals.

These key forums should have established standards and all the normal documentation and reporting supporting project delivery.

Specifications and requirements, scope change logs, risk registers, project plans, milestone plans, assumptions logs, issues logs, workstream reporting, and overall status reporting would all be expected. Projects can be traditional or agile in approach, with the latter supported by sprints and sprint reviews, retrospectives, and a general intention to deliver the most value as early as possible.

Internal Audit should review the overall design and operational effectiveness of the strategic change program office and challenge key logs, assumptions, and reports for reasonableness. Successful projects have a natural rhythm, supported by clear, concise assessments and status reports.

The details and reality on the ground should be reported candidly to the Project Executive or Owner. Early in my Internal Audit career, I was assigned to a longer-term engagement within a large strategic program. I used to attend the daily project meetings, which were chaired by the Project Sponsor, who set an excellent tone from the top.

The Project Executive was a tough taskmaster, yet he held himself to the same high standards. His desk was spotless every evening, with only a pen and lamp upon it. Issues and risks were tabled, and actions and ownership were agreed upon. Decisions were made based on the facts presented, transparent and open to input and challenge.

Workstream owners brought up real concerns, and there was vigorous discussion and good sharing of ideas when it came to overcoming near-term problems. Follow-up was required every day on key actions until issues were resolved. Attending these daily project meetings helped me to get into the flow of the project. Internal Audit understood the key risks, daily challenges, and progress being made. We could review and test key aspects of the change to provide assurance that the project team and Project Executive were on top of their risks and had sound control practices.

Skill Sets / Expertise

A high-performing audit team stands ready to take on any assignment, curious, critical-thinkers who problem-solve and reflect openly. Do your team members have the right mindset and competencies?

Internal Audit should review the qualifications and experience of key change management staff hired into the project team to confirm that the right skills and experience have been gathered to support the strategic change. It is critical for Internal Audit to assess any resource or skill set concerns that the Project Sponsor or team may have.

Workload is often a critical issue in multi-year strategic change programs. Key resources can become burnt out and may rotate out, change roles, or simply leave. Listening to early concerns, assessing the tone within the project team, and validating this against executive reporting is often a good way to detect emerging risks.

It is Executive Management and the board who are responsible for an organization's strategy. It is not Internal Audit's role to opine on whether the corporation is pursuing the right strategy. However, Internal Audit can understand and assess transformation risks, the quality and accuracy of reporting, the effectiveness of strategy governance, and the adaptation of change along the way to ensure the intended destination remains viable. Internal Audit's perspective can help keep the project on target and provide a needed dose of reality from time to time through an objective assessment of readiness and adequacy of plans to deliver strategic change.

It is important that we want the project to succeed and having a can-do attitude to help management overcome issues and fast-track potential solutions is one of the most useful aspects of Internal Audit's involvement in strategic change programs.

Openly discussing risk scenarios and being a voice of reasoned challenge can give Program Management encouragement. Our objectives in reviewing strategic change programs may be closer to 'help management find the optimal path to successful go-live' than formalized risk and control assessment. Employing the right mix of challenge, flexibility, and power pivots will be critical ingredients for success.

Areas Worth Reviewing in Most Strategic Projects

There are almost always different executives involved in setting a strategy versus delivering it. Both components require very different skill sets. The Project Sponsors and Executives may form the bridge between the two worlds. Internal Audit should immerse itself in key strategic projects, and the following are key areas that Internal Audit should consider for review:

- Project governance standards must be agreed upon and adhered to.
- The business case must be set forth and sufficiently challenged, vetted, and approved by the Board. It is important for Internal Audit to substantiate all assumptions and challenge viewpoints that may be stretching credibility.

- Requirements must be documented. Workstreams and milestones must be set out. Dependencies and assumptions should be identified and debated across the full team to help validate them.
- Risks and risk levels must be defined, updated, and mitigated where necessary. Project risk appetite and tolerance should also be defined to help ensure the program does not cut corners or take unnecessary risks when attempting to overcome near-term challenges.
- Roles, responsibilities, and accountabilities at all levels must be agreed upon.
- The methodology employed and the supporting delivery plan must be agreed upon, with reporting clearly defined.
- Key definitions and scoring or ratings criteria must be developed and applied.
- Key meeting forums need to be agreed upon and scheduled.
- Status reporting must be established to communicate progress, or the lack thereof, transparently.

Core Competencies

To assess a strategic project effectively, Internal Audit must have core competencies in the area that the project is intended to deliver. For example, if the project involves financial system transformation to deliver a new global general ledger platform, then Internal Audit resources must have financial reporting or finance expertise.

This ensures that Audit has an experienced voice to challenge appropriately and engage project management in relevant technical dialogue. If the Internal Audit function does not have adequate specialist skills in-house, it should co-source those skills from an external provider. While this may not be cheap, it can offer immediate expertise and give the audit credibility.

Furthermore, project management skills and know-how are a must. Strategic projects often operate like large temporary organizations, and as with all major change initiatives, daily activity levels fluctuate.

Direct Access to Project Executive(s) and Sponsor(s)

Attending the daily project meetings is critical for Internal Audit, as is attending the Steering Group and Project Executive meetings. As with interactions with the Audit Chair and Audit Committee, there should also be room for one-on-one meetings to gauge the tone from the top and to secure input on proposed or specific assurance work to be performed. Typically, Internal Audit's perspective can offer a different project view and assessment, and the Project Executive and Sponsor will likely be very interested in Internal Audit's perception of the big picture and any glaring weaknesses.

Internal Audit should have access to all project resources. Time, or more likely the distinct lack of it, is a critical constraint in delivering strategic projects. Internal Audit must flex its approach to deliver value in shorter bursts, and all work should have a forward-looking or immediacy focus. Using an agile audit methodology, or at least some of its key components such as sprints, can help focus on project risks and enable agreement on rapid improvements or actions to keep the project on track.

For strategic project audits, health checks, or Go/No Go assessments, Internal Audit should flex its product agility and use an approach that is fit for purpose. For large projects, it may take the form of a series of health check audits performed a couple of sprints at a time, each one focused and quite intense, ensuring the level of challenge is right and the review is both focused and forward-looking.

There should be much more anticipation in strategic project audits: what could go wrong? What risks could be outsized? What risk scenarios could apply? How would the project team recover from a failed delivery? Bringing expertise to the table and using it to challenge key aspects of the strategic change project is an effective way for Internal Audit to add value.

It is also critical to be reasonable about documentation in projects. Yes, minimum standards should be met, but expecting more and more documentation is not a useful audit observation. Indeed, many excellent strategic change teams I have observed all had one thing in common: an excellent Project Executive who clearly and concisely owned the risks. Team and Project Executive interactions were open, honest, and candid; problems were not problems for long because everyone was in solutions mode.

There was great respect among the team members and the Project Executive, and it showed. The project team was on the same page every day, and it showed. They kept project documentation lean but took great pride in solving problems and completing tasks to the highest possible standard. Nobody wanted to be the weak link or let the Project Executive down.

Focusing on current project risks relative to appetite is a great way to determine overall project health. As with more permanent interdepartmental activities and processes, risks often crystallize at handoff points within projects, and this is a worthy area of focus for Internal Audit. Discussing both current and forward-looking project risks with the project manager is an effective way to deliver meaningful challenge.

Internal Audit should facilitate discussions around project risk scenarios and develop or adapt these through critical thinking. These workshops are highly valuable and should provide assurance to the project team. Applying structure and critical thinking helps ensure that these sessions are productive and may help identify gaps in risk coverage or unexpected risk correlations.

Strategic projects can benefit greatly when Internal Audit works alongside Operational Risk, Compliance, and business governance partners. Sharing perspectives and combining challenges through integrated health checks can add substantial value to strategic project delivery. Strategic projects can fail for many reasons, and it is important to have different assurance functions around the table to challenge plans, assumptions, steps, and timeframes.

Choosing the right time to perform assurance work on strategic initiatives is also key. You do not want to be too early, and equally, you do not want to be too late. There must be enough time for management to assess corrective actions and build related solutions into their delivery plans to help keep the overall project on track.

Another key reality of strategic projects is that the end state almost always iterates and adapts along the journey. This is quite normal and reflects management making change requests as scope, technology, or delivery timeframes evolve. Audit can focus on these larger changes and review processes to identify, challenge, debate, fund, and approve or reject key changes. There should be a logical flow of analysis, management forum debate, and discussion to support such changes. These will likely trigger updates to risks, assumptions, dependency logs, sprints, or workstream plans.

A key set of constituents for Internal Audit to spend time with is the middle management team, typically the key people involved in leading or coordinating each project workstream. The tone in the middle is a good predictor of overall project health.

In my experience, effective project teams communicate well across workstream boundaries. Awareness of risks, incidents, or changes in approach or assumptions is taken seriously.

It is worthwhile for Internal Audit to spend time with each workstream head or deputy to gauge their upstream dependencies and to assess their key inputs, assumptions, handoffs, risks, and deliverables. The people in the middle are often the most aware of outsized risks and issues, so discussing the risks or surprise outcomes they foresee and devoting time to understanding the root causes and possible workarounds will enable more impactful Internal Audit reporting.

As time is of the essence, any key points should be openly discussed with project management, and once validated, action steps should be swift. The quality of the dialogue with key project owners and the value of their perceptions are what truly matter. In the best teams, you will find a shared sense of purpose and commitment across groups to help achieve strategic goals. If you do not sense that, then something is likely wrong. Perhaps a surprise outcome or a unit or end-to-end testing failure needs to be aired and discussed more broadly.

When I managed a very large project while working outside of Internal Audit, midway through my career, I quickly realized that testing (unit, end-to-end, user acceptance testing, all the components required to ensure a quality production deliverable) often gets squeezed as delivery deadlines approach. Without fail, the proposed testing window would be shortened by a week, then two, and so on.

This is a very critical area that Internal Audit should test and assess rigorously. Is it better to delay delivery by a month, or to claim victory by pushing a substandard product into production? Perfection is not the expectation in most organizations, but tensions can run high in these situations. Go or No Go? Red or green, with no in-between? Key decisions must be made. Will the documented criteria be followed, or will normal standards be abandoned in pursuit of a win?

In the end, responsibility for such decisions rightfully rests with management and the board. Internal Audit can provide objective insights and feedback on Go or No Go readiness, but we must defer the decision to our stakeholders. Management and the board ultimately own the risks.

Recap of Key Learnings in this Chapter:

1. Assess that the Program Governance Office and Program Steering Board have been established and resourced with suitably skilled professionals.

2. Few people excel in strategic competency, setting out the big picture while also excelling in project execution and delivery. Internal Audit can help bridge these different competencies by providing forward-looking assurance.

3. Internal Audit can add value by performing shorter, more focused reviews of strategic change delivery in their organizations. Time is of the essence, and review results must be shared as close to real-time as possible.

4. Internal Audit can strengthen its credibility by reviewing strategic projects with expert skill sets in the relevant area. This may require some teams to co-source specialized expertise.

5. Internal Audit's access to and relationships with the Project Sponsor and Project Delivery Executive are of critical importance. These meetings should be scheduled and conducted in an open, honest, and candid manner.

Chapter 12

AUDIT QUALITY ASSURANCE
Dynamics Beyond Ticking and Tying

Audit quality assurance, at its core, is less about how we meet standards and more about how our teams evolve, collaborate, and strive for excellence.

Most of us who have worked in larger Internal Audit teams can relate to being advised that your audit has been selected for a quality assurance review or 'QAR.' Great, I might as well just go to my dentist for an early afternoon root canal. That's often the first thought that enters your brain. Why is that?

Joking aside, I worked with some great quality assurance professionals over my career. They were all experienced auditors who knew what good looked like and took pride in challenging us, on each key aspect of the selected audit. I would not expect any more, to be honest. Reviewing audit files, team alignment, and behaviors, relative to our audit methodology is a good thing. We all want to know if we stack up or not and if not, why not.

We always appreciated quality assurance reviews where the performers were reasonable and at least gave us our day in court to have our say before passing sentence. Encouraging open, transparent discussions across quality assurance topics and reviews among our team was very important.

While some auditors may have made mistakes, sometimes there are subtleties that need to be understood, such as misinterpretations or asking for advice but not fully understanding the suggested approach. These are not excuses, but context that may help explain overall auditor intent, even if execution failed the test.

To me, the big picture was always important. First, did the team adhere to our audit methodology, and did I, as the head of the team, guide them appropriately and document any key decisions and any scope changes or deviations from our normal practice?

Secondly, were the audit workpapers logical, and did they pass the independent sniff test? Could our experienced reviewers read through the files, re-perform the audit work, and reach the same conclusions as the audit team? These are core outcomes that every audit team should want to know.

For me as a Chief Audit Executive, I was involved in every audit, not so much in the workpapers as I became more of an executive leader, but actively involved in shaping our audit methodology, finalizing key audit documents, participating in key meetings, and helping refine key messages (sprint reviews, audit comments, audit reports, and insight memoranda). As a team, we spent many hours discussing observations, approaches to testing, validity of outcomes, and any follow-on work expected to help us reach valid conclusions. I was always a talker. I loved to discuss things openly and was not particularly wedded to my own views, especially if I heard something better from one of the team members, and many times I did.

For us, the real value of a sound quality assurance philosophy is continuous learning and instilling best practices within the team. We were an agile team, and our motto was we succeed together, and we fail together. A tough QAR held our feet to the fire. Nobody wanted to be the one who let the team down. Equally, as all workpapers were peer- or manager-reviewed, I was ultimately responsible for deciding whether observations were report-worthy.

It was a multi-faceted approach, and we all had skin in the game. Irrespective of the outcome, we all wanted to feel that we were treated fairly and professionally and that any learning was meaningful and worthwhile. Transparency was the name of the game. We did not want to be roasted for relatively minor points; no toothpicks, please, as we were all under pressure sprint after sprint to deliver value.

Auditors never like to be audited, isn't that the truth? Subliminal messaging aside, QARs can be extremely good coaching and learning opportunities for the entire team, the Chief Audit Executive included. If my team failed, then we all failed, simply put. The buck stops with the head of the team, in my case, me.

Our quality assurance team used to share best practices and periodically dropped into the team mid-sprint to check in and see if there were any areas where they could help, clarify reasonable expectations, and reinforce desired standards of work. Our team appreciated that, as our quality assurance colleagues were trying to help us.

If a team member did not know the exact standard process or requirement, our quality assurance colleagues were happy to provide coaching in the field. The team would always seek advice and ask questions along the way to ensure we were interpreting steps and standards correctly.

Inevitably, if a formal QAR was announced, we would not be overly surprised. They are simply a fact of life in a large audit team. Our collective pride was at stake, and it was always good to see the team members being proactive, sharing perspectives with each other, and generally feeling comfortable being challenged.

For me as the leader, it was as much about how the team behaved and reacted to some tough questions as whether we ultimately passed, needed improvement, or failed. The analogies to how we audited business management, and their self-assessments and behaviors, certainly resonate. Importantly, it is probably fair not to expect perfection. Perfection has a very expensive price tag.

If audit files are expected to be flawless, our collective productivity would suffer. We should strive to be good to great in every audit. That is a given. But equally, we need to be mindful that quality assurance does not set an expectation of perfection, given its costs. Understanding timing pressures and our desire to be agile and efficient must be factored in, not as big excuses but as reasonableness guardrails within the quality assurance assessment process.

As a progressive Internal Audit function, our Quality Assurance team also performed several thematic reviews, covering all audits in a year or a quarter to assess the bigger picture. This is a great way to deliver broader quality assurance across key parts of the audit methodology or charter. One example was reviewing a sample of our insights memos, which were positioned not as control issues but as opportunities to consider doing something different, commercial, cultural, or efficiency related.

Our Quality Assurance team would assess whether any insights were softened reportable control issues, lest we might be arbitraging our more formal audit reports for insights that were optional for management to debate and action further. That challenge was fair and a worthy piece of thematic work to keep us all accountable.

Of interest was that our average insights feedback scores were typically higher than our audit feedback scores. While we gathered both sets of feedback scores in the same document, it is perhaps indicative of the value that Internal Audit can generate from just providing feedback on opportunities in the normal course of business.

Other thematic reviews could focus on adherence to policy or methodology changes, for example, better use of root causes in audit comments or thematic commentary from management across all our feedback forms. Reflecting on a mix of audit-specific feedback and broader departmental feedback was a big plus.

Learning was valuable for the team, regardless of whether it came from a specific audit file or a broader thematic work product. Getting this balance right is important for Internal Audit quality assurance teams to invest time in and achieve. For us, we appreciated our Quality Assurance team participating in our regular monthly meetings.

It was great to have a standing agenda item for quality assurance learnings, and this informal feedback really helped foster a professional style in our team where everybody took ownership, and we had leadership from every seat. Our quality assurance team would present recent QAR results, tips and tricks for the audit team, and the most recent thematic review, which they tried to do once every quarter or so.

As the regional Chief Audit Executive, I always supported our quality assurance team and thanked them for their work and feedback. Sometimes we had to lick our wounds when we did not earn the full passing grade, we all wanted, but then again, those mistakes would never be repeated. To err is to be human, as the old saying goes. We faced challenges at times, driven by our pace of change.

We were a very progressive audit team; we performed largely full data audits using hypotheses to test full populations. We had migrated from being a traditional annual planning team to a globally agile team, and agile adoption required quite a bit of flexing of our audit methodology. All the changes were valuable, and we all learned along the way.

Our quality assurance team provided sound support for us throughout. They were not overly rigid and recognized that it usually takes a few turns of the crank to smooth out the kinks in the chain. We appreciated that touch, not being soft but having some empathy and helping us more in the field and in real time when aspects of our work or methodology standards were new.

Our quality assurance team also played some important strategic roles. One, they helped our global head ensure our quarterly self-assessment reflected our key risks and controls. Was our risk assessment complete? Did we adhere to our audit methodology and resulting issue and report rating scales? Did Internal Audit evidence its work and key judgments and outcomes? Did we have any self-identified weaknesses, and did we need to open any action plans in the Group's Enterprise Risk system?

Answering all these questions is why you need great quality assurance talent. They play the ultimate devil's advocate role to ensure our work is effective, valuable, and achieves the appropriate standards.

Another vital role for a quality assurance team is helping ensure that Internal Audit is ready when it is time for the external QAR, required every five years pursuant to the standards of the Institute of Internal Auditors.[53] Most Internal Audit executives shudder when they hear these words. An inner voice may be saying, "Oh no, has it really been five years already, and are we even close to being ready?"

Our quality assurance team started preparing for the external QA well over a year in advance. While their work was ongoing, they always ensured they had performed a rigorous self-assessment to IIA standards and reviewed any exceptions or perceived weaknesses very closely with the global leadership team in Internal Audit to validate any suggested changes and actions required. We often asked what our peers did. Did anyone else interpret

---

53 The Institute of Internal Auditors. *International Standards for the Professional Practice of Internal Auditing (Standards)*. Lake Mary, FL: The Institute of Internal Auditors, 2017.

things the way we did? Having a strong peer network is a great way to gain perspective on more technical Internal Audit topics. Indeed, for us, it was often just a matter of being reminded what good looks like and what great looks like.

Did our quarterly self-assessments stand up to detailed review? Could we show strong evidence supporting our own controls' performance and review, and at the right time? Did we follow our own training days-per-person policy? If not, who was short of days or hours, and what was the plan? Should we have some additional mandatory training on emerging risk topics?

Equally, having a team focused objectively on our value delivery and Internal Audit's own strategy delivery is a great asset to have. In our case, it meant demonstrating progress toward our stated vision statement. As an Internal Audit Executive, it is so important to take a step back and look at the dance floor.

Being self-aware and asking objectively whether we had packaged our work and metrics appropriately helped us focus on the most important deliverables. Let's face it: we should not expect perfection. As one board member used to always remind us, "Perfection has a price; it is expensive, and most of us cannot afford it."

Good to great should be good enough. The same was true for Internal Audit. Despite a 30-day report issuance rule from the end of the last sprint, we always had some reports earlier and some later; on average, we were compliant with our target, which was good enough.

You Are What You Measure

I recall one very senior executive setting a high bar when I supported a fixed income sales team. The head of trading asked each of the trading desk managers to come to the management off-site with their strategic plans. The only catch was that it had to be no more than two pages. He wanted to really know the actions planned and how each team could demonstrate progress toward getting there through basic measures and metrics. Genius. He dispensed with all the fluff and got down to what each team would do and, by implication, what he would be measuring their success by.

It really sharpened the team's focus to deliver growth and demonstrate practical measures of success along the path to getting there. Boiling complex regional and global businesses down to a few bullet points must have been a daunting challenge, but it helped focus management on the key measures of success underpinning their growth ambitions.

Internal Audit faces similar challenges. We need to be clear that the metrics we track make sense to our Audit Committee. Establishing key metrics that are shaped by value is a real art. Indeed, there are audit departments that have great metrics but may still struggle to add value to their organizations.

Metrics need to be meaningful and convey a clear story. For example, if a department fails on average to issue reports within 30 days from the end of the last sprint (or end of fieldwork for traditional audit teams), then the Chief Audit Executive and Audit Committee should be looking deeper at the data behind the metrics.

It could be that all reports take over 30 days, and that would be a poor outcome. It could also be that satisfactory audit reports typically go out in 30 days, but unsatisfactory reports take more time. The latter may be acceptable if the extra effort is spent syndicating management action plans for important issues raised by Internal Audit in the audit reports.

Striking the right balance between input, activity, and output metrics is important. We had all the usual suspects: time to issue reports after the last sprint (30-day rule), ratings distributions, headcount versus budget, and production versus administrative hours.

Interestingly, it was qualitative feedback that proved to be a better measure of our success. Did our stakeholders feel we had the right plans in each quarterly audit plan, and how did we cover key risk themes? Did management feel engaged in our audits and receive value for money? Were our insights valuable to the business? Did we host as many guest auditors as we had planned? Could we demonstrate strategic project closures and put agreed changes in place to realize our vision?

We found that delivering an annual state of the union update to all our Audit Committees and Board stakeholders was a great way to showcase all that we had delivered, what we were still working on as a global function, and our vision for where we were going (looking out a year or two ahead). While not a formal QAR deliverable, such a strategic paper was worth its weight in gold.

It was cohesive, strategic, and forward-looking. It was a terrific marketing piece for our function, and of course, it was easy to digest and relate to. Those performing our external QAR loved these annual pieces, as they really demonstrated our executive commitment to high standards and our progress as a function in an overarching way. Who wouldn't be interested in an executive report like that?

Smaller and mid-sized audit teams face the challenge that they may not have full-time QAR resources. Fractional quality assurance resources from co-source providers or consultants can help, but in my experience, a lot can be accomplished just by rotating the responsibility among team members, performing objective reviews, and holding rapid improvement sessions.

Quality assurance and continuous improvement are a mindset, and following agile principles can be a great help to audit teams that cannot afford full-time quality assurance resources. The key is to be driven to improve and to scorecard key aspects of the reporting process and outcomes. Being self-critical about the story the scorecards tell is the first step toward identifying where to improve and why. That is why I love agile principles, especially using team retrospectives to reflect, learn, adjust, and grow.[54]

Quality Assurance Across the Audit Team Itself

What should we do to ensure the health of our audit teams? If you support the notion that our people are our biggest asset, then we should spend plenty of time asking for and providing feedback and ensuring the experience of working within the Internal Audit team is the optimal one, given personal objectives. As an agile and catalyst leader, having a flat, open team structure worked for me. We liked the idea of an open-mic session to kick our team meetings off. We liked having lunch together.

Globally, we encouraged skip-level meetings, but as everyone knew me, we did not need them in our team; however, we did encourage meetings with the Group Head without me. One thing that always worked for me was inviting all Internal Audit team members to lunch or drinks when I visited an overseas office, not just the people in my own team. It sounds small, but this openness created lots of friendships and goodwill. Nobody likes to be excluded, and everyone appreciates a free lunch or drink. It did not cost the company much and yet yielded a great return on investment, as they say.

---

54 Schwaber, Ken, and Jeff Sutherland. *The Scrum Guide: The Definitive Guide to Scrum: The Rules of the Game.* Scrum.org, 2020.

Having an inclusive culture is a great thing and really encourages team members to learn new things and share ideas. Collective learning contributes to a great team. There is no real magic sauce here, but the tone at the top, middle, and bottom all comes from the team leader. It is important for Chief Audit Executives to reflect and ask whether they are truly leading or simply acting as narrow-minded bosses focused on themselves and struggling for motivation. We can be liked and still be tough leaders; the key difference lies in the level of two-way respect.

A boss has little respect from their team members because they are generally fixated on their own narrow view of the world. Bosses typically embrace a rule-by-fear mentality and fail at leadership because they lack empathy and do not care much for others' opinions or views. It is probably a sad reflection, but audit teams led by bosses rather than leaders tend to implode.

Much of the audit talent will leave for greener pastures, leaving behind those who wish they could move on as well. Everybody else will be permanently walking on eggshells, just awaiting the next blow-up.

Sadly, there are Internal Audit teams that are boss-led and not leader-led. My advice is to assess whether your audit team is actively being led by a leader of people and ideas, or just a boss intent on forcing his or her view. If the latter, try not to overstay your welcome and steer well clear of leaderless leaders. You will flourish in a team where there is a leader of talent, people, and ideas.

Recap of Key Learnings in this Chapter:

1. Progressive and agile teams embrace the concept of quality assurance, as it is a great shared learning opportunity for the audit team.

2. Make quality assurance learnings and interactions a core part of your Internal Audit team meetings. Invite QA colleagues to provide updates at these meetings and encourage QA to drop into audits in real time to provide coaching in the field.

3. You are what you measure.[55] Chief Audit Executives should balance input, output, and activity-based metrics and seek qualitative feedback from key stakeholders to ensure audit work and risk coverage are valued, helping the function thrive.

4. QA teams should add value through performing a mix of broader thematic reviews across all the audits in the period under review, as well as core assessments of methodology adherence and reperformance on specific audits.

55 Austin, Robert D. *Measuring and Managing Performance in Organizations.* New York: Dorset House Publishing, 1996.

Recap of Key Learnings in this Chapter:

5. Leverage AI to augment your QA practices.[56] Tools such as a secure, corporate version of ChatGPT can help perform quality assessments and rate audit workpaper quality for methodology adherence. Indeed, AI-driven QA review may be invoked by the Internal Audit team in real time.

56 OpenAI. *ChatGPT (GPT-4) Technical Report.* San Francisco: OpenAI, 2023. https://arxiv.org/abs/2303.08774.

Chapter 13

LEADERSHIP, VISION, AND AUDIT COMMITTEES

Leadership and vision are highly sought-after and increasingly vital skills within the Internal Audit community today.

We may all have role models, both good and bad. In musical terms, when I think about leadership, I think about Bob Geldof, the organizer of Band Aid and Live Aid in the mid-eighties. A fellow Irishman, Bob Geldof, was a rock star in the late seventies and early eighties, fronting the Boomtown Rats, who had good success in the UK and Europe with songs like I Don't Like Mondays.[57] He is articulate and direct, and is well known for using expletives to make his point clear.

Many of us remember his impassioned plea during Live Aid to "Give us your f@#!ing money!"[58] Back in the eighties, cursing

57 The Boomtown Rats, *I Don't Like Mondays*, track 1 on *The Fine Art of Surfacing*, Ensign Records, 1979.

58 *Live Aid*. "Bob Geldof Urges Donations." Broadcast July 13, 1985. BBC Television, London.

on live TV was simply not done. Yet despite the initial shock and outcry, Bob's words were the right ones at the right time. Charitable donations flooded in from ordinary people, perhaps sensing the desperation in his voice as he urged support for the starving people of Ethiopia. The rest is history.[59]

Colorful language aside, Bob Geldof demonstrated great leadership. He saw the television reports about the famine in Ethiopia and, fed up with political inaction, took it upon himself to do something to draw attention to the suffering and inhumanity. I doubt he ever expected to galvanize the music world globally into supporting him in recording songs to raise money through Band Aid. Further, I doubt he expected to organize and produce the greatest global rock concerts of the modern age, with the *Live Aid* concerts in London and Philadelphia.

Bob Geldof connected well with the ordinary man and woman in the street; he meant well and had real purpose. He led his peers and created real societal value by getting so many big stars aligned and on the same page quickly. He did not do it for notoriety; he did it because he cared, and his purpose with Band Aid and *Live Aid* was so much bigger than any of his personal ambitions. The sum of the parts assembled for Band Aid and *Live Aid* greatly exceeded the contributions of any individual singer or band. An inspiring and authentic leader, he demonstrated the absolute power of shared values and objectives in realizing a dream.

Equally important, Bob Geldof had another key trait: he knew how to get things done. Presumably, long stretches on the road, playing in a different city every night, helped him build the logistical and mobilization skills that were certainly needed. His no-nonsense, hard-driving style ensured the ambitions of Band Aid and *Live Aid* were realized. His honorary knighthood

59 BBC News. "Live Aid: The Day the Music Changed the World." July 13, 2015. https://www.bbc.com/news/entertainment-arts-33476380.

is testament to his leadership skills and his ability to get the best out of people around the world.[60]

So, what can Internal Auditors learn from Bob Geldof?

No, not the tempting use of expletives to describe audits, management responses, management, or the Board, but the importance of investing in leadership skills. 'Sir Bob,' as he is often referred to, was and still is a catalyst for positive change in the world; he put his own career aside and rose to a much higher calling. By coordinating Band Aid and Live Aid he highlighted the importance of giving back and many of those musicians who performed at these events continued to actively support just social causes. Bob Geldof's passion for the cause served as a wonderful example and inspiration for many of his well-known rock musician friends and the public at large.

Indeed, his music career was never the same after *Live Aid*, and his band, The Boomtown Rats, fizzled out. Yet his impact on society lives on forty years later.[61] Giving back and extending a hand to those in need has become the norm.

Internal Audit leaders help to shape their organizations. In many respects, they play the role of the organizational conscience, assessing whether risks are understood and controlled, regulations are followed, and good outcomes are generated for clients, the business, and its employees. Empowering the Audit team to create value through their perspectives, while being objective, fair, and having integrity, are critical success factors.

---

60 The London Gazette. "Honorary Knighthood Conferred upon Bob Geldof." January 1986.

61 The Guardian. "Bob Geldof: From Punk Rocker to Humanitarian." July 12, 2020. https://www.theguardian.com/music.

Chief Audit Executives must have their teams' backs and coach them to deliver impact and value beyond any one person's capabilities. At times, we must be diplomatic, and at times we must be forthright, all the while being good sparring partners with the business to help it thrive. Like Sir Bob, Internal Auditors must garner a reputation for getting things done and delivering value on time.

Vision is another critical trait that Internal Audit leaders require, especially those who are or aspire to be in the role of Chief Audit Executive. When I think of a rock star with vision, I immediately think of David Bowie. His music, his multiple personas, his performances, and all the visuals that went along with them made him truly distinctive. He was forward-looking and never seemed to dwell on the past. He was a trailblazer, and he led while many others followed.

To an outsider like me, David Bowie epitomized continuous learning, personal growth, and evolution. His songs were all unique but instantly recognizable as Bowie, whether rock or more pop oriented. He transcended time, music, and fashion, remaining relevant to and instantly recognized by multiple generations.

One interesting case to watch on YouTube is when Jeremy Paxman, a senior BBC journalist, interviews David Bowie in the nineties about the impact of the new thing at the time called the Internet.[62] David Bowie's perspective on the societal changes the Internet would bring proved devastatingly accurate, as we can now see with twenty-five years of hindsight.[63]

---

62 BBC Newsnight. "David Bowie Predicts the Impact of the Internet." Interview by Jeremy Paxman. BBC, 1999. Available at https://www.youtube.com/watch?v=FiK7s_0tGsg.

63 Rolling Stone. "David Bowie's 1999 Internet Prediction." January 11, 2016. https://www.rollingstone.com/music.

While Jeremy Paxman is quite dismissive and suggests it is a bit of a fad, David Bowie doesn't flinch and does a terrific job outlining how the Internet would change lives, businesses, music, and the arts in ways he could not even fully imagine or describe. He had great vision, and it showed; he led, and others followed.

So, what can Internal Auditors learn from David Bowie?

We must articulate our vision clearly and pursue it with vigor. Equally, we must not shy away from the need to update and adapt our vision given continuous change in our business and technological environments.

Just as Geldof and Bowie reinvented how the world engaged with their work, Internal Audit leaders must also define a vision that reimagines their purpose and influence. Audit departments and teams continually evolve, and if technology and digitalization have taught us anything, it is not to sit still. These days (Winter 2025/6), I hope most Internal Audit teams have established a Vision statement.

I am quite sure most Audit functions in larger public companies have done so, but perhaps there is still work to do in moderate and smaller-sized teams. To have no vision implies that, as a leader, you are content to maintain the status quo. That would be a big mistake in my book, a lost opportunity. The pace of change in Internal Audit expectations and capabilities has never been greater, and if your vision lacks sufficient aspiration and ambition, you run the risk of becoming irrelevant over time.

In its simplest form, a Vision statement for an Internal Audit team is an aspirational sentence or two that describes the big picture of where the function wants to be a few years out, say three years ahead. It should be ambitious and aspirational but achievable in time with sustained effort and strategic change within the Audit function.

When we set out our first Vision statement in my previous Internal Audit team over a decade ago, it took the global leadership team nearly a day to agree on the two sentences. It took us another day to map out all the high-level changes required within Internal Audit to enable us as a team to realize our shared vision.

These were major strategic changes that we collectively believed were necessary to bring our vision to life. Interestingly, our Vision statement made no mention of the word 'audit.' It was aspirational and focused on business partnering, data analytics, critical thinking, and compelling insights, all great things for Internal Audit to aspire to.

Once we set out our vision statement, we had to map out a path to getting there. Many aspects of our organization, audit methodology, audit products, and risk culture would need to be modified, some quite substantially.

To achieve our vision, Internal Audit would need to transform itself. We brainstormed for a day and identified a series of desired changes across our function. We grouped these changes into three key buckets: People, Process (including our Internal Audit Methodology), and Products. We also added a fourth overall bucket, Culture, to capture initiatives stemming from all the strategic changes and to reflect how they interrelated. This helped ensure our team culture evolved alongside our vision journey.

Our team members volunteered to get involved in various strategic initiatives supporting the delivery of our vision. Because our team members all had full-time audit roles, change delivery became a shared endeavor carried out alongside their daily responsibilities.

Establishing project charters for each initiative was a great help to keep us honest and on track. We would hold an off-site meeting every six months to assess our progress and tackle any setbacks or redirections required. Team members participated selectively to ensure we had grassroots and tone-from-the-middle input and feedback.

Setting our vision and delivering the changes needed to achieve it took eighteen months to two years of effort, but we got into a great rhythm. After two years, we decided our current vision lacked sufficient ambition and updated it with heightened expectations for Internal Audit and the team. It was a wonderful experience that our entire global team bought into and was proud to be part of, and I would recommend this approach to any Internal Audit leader looking to develop a team vision.

In two years, we had moved the dial on our data analytics capabilities and were performing many full-data audits supported by hypothesis testing. We hired data scientists and embedded them in each of our teams. Alongside our audit reports, we shared compelling insights with management; these were well received, and over time, many in management came to value our insights even more than the formal audit reports. The law of unintended consequences, I suppose, but we increasingly found our voice and shared informal perspectives more openly with management, and they genuinely appreciated it.

We were a fluid department with ongoing changes. Newness and fresh ideas abounded. Our team became more empowered, and that eagerness to promote change from within to add value created the right atmosphere for staff to raise suggestions and new ideas. Our whole world became quite a virtuous circle, and our audit function progressed forward at speed and together. The only constant in our Internal Audit team was change itself. Reflecting on all the strategic changes we made, the journey was, in many respects, as valuable as the destination.

Illustration 3: Internal Audit Vision North Star Chart

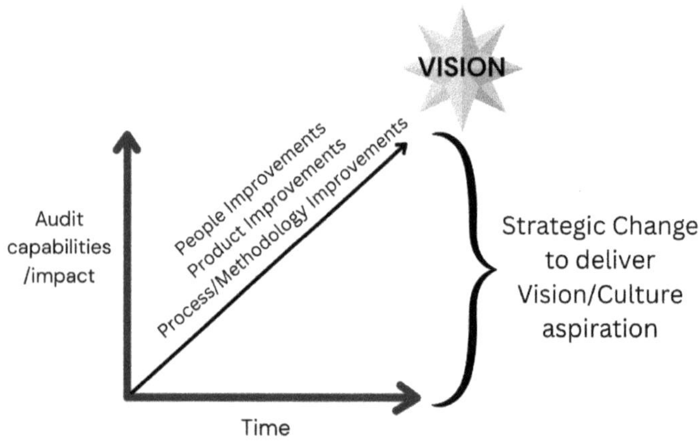

The chart reflects the increased value that can accrue to Internal Audit over time by focusing delivery of people, product and audit methodology changes aligned to your Internal Audit Vision. The journey towards realizing the team's aspirational vision will unlock value and increase Internal Audit's value to the organization.

Demonstrating Audit Committee Leadership

Audit Committees can be the ultimate test of an Internal Auditor's knowledge, risk awareness, judgment, and communication skills. They are great learning fora, as non-executive directors with varying expertise and Executive Management come together to take stock of business, financial, Internal Audit, and other assurance activities.

Never go into the Audit Committee thinking you can just wing it; always be prepared for the unexpected. It is critical to know your audience and having an open and honest pre-meeting with the Audit Committee Chair is among the best preparation steps to take to bring your A game.

For a musical analogy, I think about two rock stars, Freddie Mercury of Queen and the great blues guitarist Albert Collins. Freddie Mercury was a natural when it came to knowing his audience. He would get them involved in the middle of or between songs and have them participate, repeating back his words and notes in a game. Audiences loved it. Everyone felt he was involving them personally. It's no wonder Freddie is often described as the greatest frontman in rock music.

Albert Collins had a completely different audience engagement style, although it was equally effective. Albert was affectionately known in the music world as 'The Master of the Telecaster,' given his expert playing of his Fender Telecaster guitar. Unusually, he played his guitar without a pick and had a masterful vibrato to accentuate notes and chords.

Collins' normal performance antics included playing guitar with an exceedingly long electric cable so he could walk down into his audience while playing, sometimes even sitting down in the middle of the crowd while still playing and keeping perfect time with his band, The Ice Breakers. He could bend notes and chords to sound out phrases like 'thank you.' It was a sight to behold and, of course, electrified his audiences. All eyes were on Albert, and he might stand up and play the guitar behind his head for good measure.

Both Freddie Mercury and Albert Collins performed at *Live Aid* in 1985.[64] Queen performed a few songs at Wembley Stadium to great acclaim, marking a comeback for Freddie Mercury, who was not well. Albert made a guest appearance with George Thorogood and the Destroyers in Philadelphia; in the middle of

---

64 *Live Aid* Official Website. "Live Aid Lineup 1985." Accessed July 10, 2025. https://www.liveaid.fandom.com.

one song, Madison Blues,[65] he was welcomed on stage, plugged in his trusty Fender Telecaster, and played the lead guitar part for a few minutes.[66]

One hundred and twenty thousand fans were in awe of his blues-rock licks; he walked on, delivered the goods, took a bow, and exited the stage gracefully. That is how it is done: be executive, deliver the goods, take a bow, and be cool.

The Chair of your Audit Committee is probably your most important relationship, and it is critical that you get to know your Audit Committee Chair and openly discuss emerging risk topics, audit results and issues, business insights, management and business changes, and the audit department vision, journey, and team.

The Audit Committee Chair and the Committee members will really value candid discussion of the audit results and ratings in the period, as well as a forward-looking view on risk. For me, we always used our pre-meeting with the Audit Committee Chair to outline our key points while asking the Chair for any topics or risks they wanted us to broach in the meeting. Conducting these pre-meetings a couple of weeks before the Audit Committee session helped us focus our messaging and refine the likely content of our update.

Now, every Board is different. In large organizations, Audit Committees tend to have a lot of participants and speakers. The full Board can be eight or ten executives, plus Executive Management, and the rest of us, invited to provide updates. Big Boards can be intimidating; rule of thumb, speak when you are spoken to, unless you have some specific data point that may be helpful.

65 *Madison Blues*, composed by Elmore James and performed by George Thorogood and The Destroyers accompanied by Albert Collins.

66 *George Thorogood and the Destroyers: Live Aid Performance*, Philadelphia, 1985. *Live Aid Archive Video*, accessed July 10, 2025. https://www.youtube.com/watch?v=c4zCzYsyJZQ.

As a guest speaker, there needs to be a certain corporate respect for how Board and Audit Committee meetings are run. We had sufficient time to provide our updates on Internal Audit results, coverage of key risk themes, our audit plans and forward-looking views of risks. Private sessions were typically part of our Audit Committee updates too, and these were typically organized in turn between the Audit Committee members, firstly with management, then with the external auditors, then with Risk Management and Compliance and finally with Internal Audit.

I always found the private sessions useful, not because of any great secrets we shared but because they were down-to-earth, quick chats about anything pressing or any additional perspective to share on specific audit reports or relevant topics. It was always good to be prepared and have two or three points to raise. Our Audit Committee members were typically very engaging and appreciated insights and context that helped their understanding. After all, in many respects we were their eyes and ears.

As an agile audit team, we presented quarterly audit plans and our coverage of emerging risk topics was very much here and now, typically in the following quarterly plan or even the current quarter. Maintaining great relationships with management ensured that Internal Audit could gather many relevant business and risk updates and form views on areas or risk themes that were bubbling to the surface. Our Audit Committees loved this, and they periodically requested coverage of specific risk themes, legal entities, or specific business scopes.

Despite the organizational hierarchy, we operated as partners. We also presented an updated view of forward-looking audits we were considering for future quarters presented under our Key Risk Themes; Annually we agreed with the Audit Committee and Executive Board four or five key risk themes including some strategic / Group themes to ensure our audit coverage was mapped largely to risks that really mattered to our organization and Board.

While we hardened our audit plan views quarterly, the forward-looking view was a great tool to prompt Audit Committee feedback and discussion, particularly on rationale, feedback from Audit Committee members and some new suggestions. Our prep work always paid off as our forward-looking audit view (soft pipeline) prompted conversation around the table.

While there is no one-size-fits-all formula for Audit Committee update materials, our materials typically included:

- Overall control environment assessment.
- Recent audit results, with a focus on any unsatisfactory or surprising outcomes.
- Year-to-date and prior-year summary tables covering audit ratings, risk culture ratings, and residual risk ratings.
- Tables outlining the number and ratings of open issues by business area, including any items past due.
- Reopened issues based on Internal Audit testing of issues closed by management and any repeat audit comments.
- Quarterly audit plan with supporting rationale (typically one or two sentences supporting each proposed audit).
- Key Risk Themes update, including audits completed, in progress, and future audits being considered, mapped to respective themes, along with key metrics related to Internal Audit impact and work delivery.
- Appendix with detailed tables showing statistics for each audit report issued year-to-date by business unit and ratings.

Presentation style can be another way to bring out your inner Internal Audit rock star when in front of the Audit Committee or Board. In Audit Committee presentations, it takes real discipline to avoid diving too deeply into detail. We all know most Internal Auditors love to talk about audits, results, ratings, and key themes.

It is important to remember that your Audit Committee and Executive Management participants have already pre-read your materials. I learned from some of the best Chief Audit Executives in the business: keep it at a high level, make your key points, then stop and take questions from the committee members. Be executive, and it will pay off.

I always wrote out my presentation notes the day before and practiced my lines a few times. Getting the right speed of delivery, tone, and pitch is important, and I always felt confident delivering my key messages, even if at times it felt like the lion's den. Interestingly, most of the time when it came time to provide my updates to the Audit Committee, I was on autopilot and felt comfortable just checking off each heading from my prepared notes for completeness. Having presented to many Audit Committees in the United States, Canada, the UK, Ireland, and Switzerland, taking this approach always worked well for me.

Your delivery pace is critical to maintaining audience interest; at all costs, do not talk slowly, and even worse, do not read from a script. There is nothing worse stylistically at the Audit Committee. For a time, our Internal Audit update followed a very slow, methodical speaker from a different assurance function. The person was very capable and performed good work, but you could feel the room tense up as people lost interest, took bathroom breaks, or became visibly restless. Their body language said it all.

As a practical matter, avoid droning on in a monotone voice when updating the Audit Committee or Board, believing you are indispensable. Doing that is a recipe for disaster. The only upside for me in following a speaker like that was that my updates, being executive (largely taking the materials as read) and relatively fast-paced, made me look great in front of the Audit Committee.

With Audit Committee meetings sometimes running three to four hours, having good executive delivery will be appreciated. Of course, the Audit Committee members will devote as much time as they want to the Internal Audit slot. Invariably, you will be asked a question that you cannot answer fully or directly; the best approach is to note the question and agree to revert to that Audit Committee member or the full Committee with a written response in a relatively short timeframe. Personally, I liked the reputation of being a closer: get in, deliver the goods, get out, and avoid losing your head in the process. Very Albert Collins.

In some Audit Committees, we tended to be toward the end of the meeting agenda, and sometimes the meeting might run late. The Audit Committee Chair always knew that I could give them back five to ten minutes by being executive. Not getting between Audit Committee members and their scheduled lunch, of course, may be a better way to describe the value there!

Beyond the Audit Committee meetings themselves, one strategy that worked very well for us was to periodically have the Audit Committee Chair or members meet with the Audit team. In our case, we scheduled dinner for our UK team, plus the Department Heads from Compliance and Operational Risk (our Coordinated Assurance Partners) and the two Audit Committee Chairs (covering different affiliated insurance carriers).

These informal dinners were terrific events. The audit team loved the fact that they were meeting their ultimate stakeholders, and the messaging and banter from the Audit Committee Chairs were fun and inspiring. Hearing powerful messages such as "be our eyes and ears," "audit with purpose," and "deliver your insights so management will appreciate them" greatly strengthened our team's esprit de corps. This feedback and direct connection with the Audit Committee members spurred the audit team to be more commercially focused and, I would say, better at handling management challenges.

Whether you are inspiring change like Geldof, envisioning the future like Bowie, or commanding attention like Mercury, the true leader in Internal Audit knows the art of influence, vision, and informal value delivery.

Connecting the audit team periodically with the Audit Committee was a win-win strategy and helped bridge the gap between the audit performers and reviewers and those who use our reports as critical corporate governance and stewardship tools.

Another very positive interaction for the entire Audit Department was to have the Chair of our Group Audit Committee join our team off-site for half a day. Again, the opportunity for Internal Audit to connect informally, share ideas, and hold a question-and-answer session was great. The Audit team was left invigorated and inspired by a Board member who absolutely relied upon the quality of its work every day.

Recap of Key Learnings in this Chapter:

1. Leaders within Internal Audit must be catalysts for positive organizational change.

2. Catalyst and servant leadership styles within Internal Audit will help the audit team add value greater than the sum of the individual parts. Internal Audit leaders must care about the business and want the business to thrive.[67]

3. An aspirational vision for Internal Audit is a great way to align and empower the Audit team to deliver strategic change over a multi-year timeframe.

4. Developing strategic change initiatives grouped under People, Product, Process (including Audit Methodology), and Culture provides an executable roadmap for transforming your team and achieving your vision.[68]

5. Revisit your vision statement every six months to assess progress, address challenges, and make refinements. Find ways to have your team

67 Bradberry, Travis. "Catalyst Leadership: Inspiring Change and Growth." *Harvard Business Review*, May 12, 2019.

68 Kotter, John P. *Leading Change*. Boston: Harvard Business School Press, 1996.

Recap of Key Learnings in this Chapter:

participate in validating and delivering your strategic initiatives.

6. In delivering your vision for your Internal Audit team, the journey is often as, or more, valuable an experience as the ultimate destination. Change is the only constant, so enjoy the ride, but never become complacent. Once you feel like you are close to achieving your vision, it is probably time to heighten your ambition and aspiration levels and embark on a new vision journey.

7. Be well-prepared for delivering Audit Committee updates and be ready to wow your audience like Freddie Mercury and Albert Collins did.

8. Be executive in the content you choose to highlight from your report and keep a relatively fast pace to instill confidence.

9. Develop key risk and strategic themes with your Audit Committee and Executive Management team, and map audits executed, in progress, and being considered for the future (Internal Audit's forward-looking view) against these thematic headings.

Chapter 14

GREAT INTERNAL AUDITOR SUPERPOWERS: SALES, RELATIONSHIPS, NETWORKING, AND CREATIVE INFLUENCING

Let's be honest. Sales skills and creativity may not always come naturally to members of the Internal Audit community. We often view ourselves as thorough, persistent, independent, and challenging types, and I could keep going with strong, inquisitive adjectives. Why is that? Why don't Internal Auditors and Chief Audit Executives focus on and devote more time to developing sales and relationship skills? We are all human, after all.

Can we honestly expect to reach our full potential and impact if we sit back and look at the historic status quo, the veil of independence and anonymity, to be our corporate salvation?

One of the greatest skills that Internal Auditors can possess is selling (and subsequently performing) the right audit at the right time to management, the Audit Committee, and the Board. However, as we all know, that is not an easy task. Having a seat at the big table requires Chief Audit Executives and their teams to constantly juggle priorities, deliver the right messages, remain tough yet fair, and keep the organization's risk and control framework moving forward.

Delivering commercial value and impact is a must for Internal Audit teams. To do this consistently, while also being a trusted advisor, requires immense sales and relationship skills, particularly at the Chief Audit Executive level and among their direct reports.

You do not need to be an accountant to be an effective Internal Auditor. Effectiveness is driven by having the right mindset to add value, being professionally skeptical, commercial, and fair. That said, most accountants and Internal Auditors love structure: templates to be completed, balances and differences to be extrapolated, and, of course, conclusions to be reached. There is nothing wrong with that.

As a Chartered Accountant with three decades in external and Internal Audit roles, I can relate to that. Those types of activities formed a fair bit of my collective experience and, no shocker, I was pretty good at them too. However, my 'aha' moments came when I worked in roles outside of audit mid-way through my career. I worked in various E-Commerce, Strategic Projects, and Fixed Income Coverage Strategy roles.

When you work outside of Internal Audit, you need to cultivate relationships more proactively. It is push and pull. Demonstrating and selling your relevance becomes your calling card. "What can I do for you?" becomes an obvious question. "What do we have in common, and how can we exchange ideas or demonstrate relevance?" also become important relationship-opening points. Internal Auditors, by design, always have doors open for them by the nature of their roles.

What executive or manager will not make time for Internal Audit, knowing the consequences of potential negative feedback if they are perceived to be uncooperative or dismissive of risk and internal controls assessment?

Subliminally, Internal Auditors devote a lot of time to activities that require active selling and relationship management expertise to add value to the Board, Audit Committee, and Executive Management. These activities, at their core, require creativity, open-mindedness, and at times a sense of fun and lightheartedness. Don't take yourself too seriously, and you might just identify great opportunities hiding in plain sight.

Comradery, Fun and Unbridled Creativity: A Flock of Seagulls and the Most Iconic Eighties Haircut

We all make mistakes, even Internal Auditors. We all know some colleagues who tend to jump to early conclusions, not actively listening or corroborating fact patterns, and so on. Equally, we all know auditors who simply like to plod along, sticking to a well-tested script while auditing on autopilot. They are slaves to the process and lack creativity.

We all need to learn from our mistakes and try not to repeat them, and this is well-worn ground, to be honest. But what if your mistake or creativity turns out to be more valuable in the long run? You may have stumbled into something new. Well, that's what happened in the early eighties to a band called Flock of Seagulls.

They were a group of hairdressers from Liverpool, England, who had formed a band and were pretty good.[69] Who doesn't like their mega-hit I Ran (So Far Away)? They were pioneers of the early synthesizer sound that the eighties is now famous for. In the VH1 television 2004 production of *Bands Reunited*, it

69 A Flock of Seagulls, *I Ran (So Far Away)*, released July 1982, Jive Records.

is explained that while joking around cutting the lead singer's hair, one of his bandmates and fellow barber jokingly brushed his hair upwards on the sides.[70] (I would describe the haircut as having a long fringe in the front, long hair in the back, and the sides brushed and held straight up.) And just like that, the now-infamous Flock of Seagulls haircut was born. While an iconic haircut might seem a far cry from the world of internal auditing, this story reminds us that sometimes playfulness and spontaneity can spark breakthroughs that structured processes alone can never produce.

Motörhead's Trail-Blazing Double Bass Drum Beat and Ronnie James Dio's Maloik!

Sometimes ordinary people do extraordinary things without knowing it, at the time. Seemingly small acts or changes in practices can resonate and drive immense value and change over the long term. As internal auditors, we actively pursue continuous improvement, applying best practices and conducting sprint retrospectives to reflect, learn and progress. The stories of Motörhead and Ronnie James Dio, remind us that 'next level' innovation and impact often hide in plain sight.

In 1978, the British heavy metal band Motörhead went into the studio to record their second album Overkill. The title song *Overkill* set the bar for a whole new genre of music, thrash metal.[71] Little did Motörhead's drummer Phil Taylor know at the time,

70 *Bands Reunited*, season 1, episode "A Flock of Seagulls," directed by Han Kim, aired February 2004, VH1.

71 Motörhead, *Overkill*, released March 24, 1979, Bronze Records.

but he was about to unleash a drumming style that would become a cornerstone of modern thrash metal. Phil was the first drummer to use double bass drums across an entire song, thus creating that fast, hypnotic drumbeat that is at the core of most thrash bands today.

As Motörhead's guitarist 'Fast' Eddie Clarke noted, he and Lemmy had returned to the studio and heard Phil playing double bass drums (foot drums) on his new drum kit as he warmed up.[72] They told him to keep that beat going because musically the beat had something, as they picked up their guitars. The rest is history. Motörhead's Overkill drumbeat was a game changer, and Phil Taylor is revered among heavy metal drummers worldwide for laying down a beat that is widely emulated today.

Ronnie James Dio was the lead singer in several big hard rock and heavy metal bands dating back to the seventies, including Rainbow, Black Sabbath, Heaven & Hell, and Dio. Known for his amazing vocal range and diminutive stature, Ronnie had another claim to fame, or should we say his grandmother did.

As a kid, Ronnie's grandma used to make a hand gesture to him called the 'maloik'[73] to protect him by warding off evil or the evil eye. It was formed by raising your index finger and pinkie finger with your middle two fingers in the palm of your hand and your thumb on top of your second finger. Ronnie used to make this hand gesture at shows, and before long it became the hand symbol of choice for rock concertgoers expressing their satisfaction with the music and show.[74] Rock on!

---

72 "Interview with 'Fast' Eddie Clarke," *Classic Rock Magazine*, issue 128 (2009).

73 Dio, Ronnie James. Interview in *A Metalhead's Journey*. "Ronnie James Dio explains the Maloik / metal horns story." YouTube video: https://www.youtube.com/watch?v=Zai16APm3Ps

74 Jon Wiederhorn, "How Ronnie James Dio Made the Devil Horns Metal's Most Iconic Hand Gesture," *Loudwire*, May 16, 2017.

So, what can Internal Auditors learn from the members of A Flock of Seagulls, Motörhead's Phil Taylor, and Ronnie James Dio?

Thankfully, I don't expect any Internal Auditors to get A Flock of Seagulls haircut anytime soon, though it might make for a fun idea to don such wigs at your next Internal Audit offsite or for your new digital meme. But their creative experimenting is worth reflecting on. Yes, they were joking around, but their creativity and spontaneity produced something iconic. That is a concept that we, as Internal Auditors, can embrace. Let's not always think we know how to solve the puzzle or have a draft answer in our pocket.

The examples of Phil and Ronnie highlight the importance of listening to feedback and acting on it and not being afraid to try new things. Equally, be yourself and don't try to be someone you are not. Phil did, and with the support of his bandmates, they recorded a great song, Overkill, with an amazing drumbeat. Without the drumming in Overkill as the leading example, we may never have had the thrash metal sounds of the eighties and beyond. Ronnie's use of the maloik hand gesture was a simple childhood response to mimic his grandmother, yet it now has universal appeal and acceptance among heavy metal concertgoers. Ronnie was just doing something that came naturally to him; he was being himself.

Sometimes, experimenting, showing creativity, and embracing informality can yield great results. So, as Internal Auditors, we should actively leverage what I call the informal audit cycle: relationships, insights, and shared calls to action across the organization in support of our more formal audit work.

Great Internal Auditors are creative and open to experimenting with testing approaches and data hypotheses. Informality is a much underused strategy by Internal Auditors. Being informal helps build trust and supports open conversations, which are critical success factors for internal auditing effectively. Don't stick rigidly to the playbook. Look for opportunities to actively engage your clients and team in conversation and share ideas and opportunities informally when you can.

Some Internal Auditors are simply afraid to share their ideas openly. They may have a great idea or insight, but rather than sharing it with management now so action can be considered or taken, they prefer to wait until their formal audit starts in six months. That way, they will have an issue for the audit report 'in the bag' right out of the gate. That approach is shortsighted and unhelpful.

Unfortunately, it still happens today in some teams. My advice to Internal Auditors is, don't subscribe to the 'gotcha mentality.' If you have something useful to say, say it; give feedback now and don't wait. Just as great music evolves through experimentation and risk-taking, Internal Audit can evolve by embracing creativity and informality to connect better with management.

Examples of Internal Audit Sales and Relationship Management Activities, Enabled by Creativity and Open Minds

1. Selling your ideas to cover the organization's key risks to improve its resilience (aka the Audit Plan resulting from your key risk assessment).
2. Selling your ideas on optimal audit or review timing and interaction with the second line or line one and a half functions (aka coordinated assurance).

3. Selling your proposed audit scope to key stakeholders (audit scope).

4. Selling your audit issues and insights identified in each audit to management and key stakeholders (aka the audit report and insights).

5. Selling the optimal way to perform audits to your audit team and stakeholders (aka the audit or agile audit methodology).

6. Selling the overarching risk and control environment messaging and audit impact every quarter to the Audit Committee and Board stakeholders (aka your Audit Committee update report). We developed an annual State of the Union Report – Internal Audit Reflection Report, which for us was a highly valued marketing document that bridged the prior year's audit coverage, issues raised, key risk themes progression, and focus going forward and strategic change within the Internal Audit function (supporting our Vision).

7. Selling your relevance and demonstrating that you care about the business being successful to management stakeholders every quarter in relationship meetings (relationship updates).

8. Selling continuous learning with your teams so that your Internal Audit team has the right skills to add value and ensuring that Internal Audit is a source of talent and a talent incubator for the organization. Selling your discipline and secret sauce to external audit so that they can feel comfortable with Internal Audit's work and having open, honest, and candid conversations with a team aligned with their external audit success and integrity.

There is no doubt about it, Internal Auditors and Chief Audit Executives are involved with selling and relationship management activities every day of the week. But being candid, some Chief Audit Executives and their teams are much better than their peers in this realm.

Unfortunately, selling has not been a skill set that Internal Auditors have historically focused on. But, as you can see from the points above, selling in all its forms is a core component of being an effective Internal Auditor. So, an obvious question to pose is whether there are practical actions that Internal Audit teams and leaders can embrace to embed sales and relationship management skills within the team. There are several key opportunities worth exploring, which I will outline below.

How to Embed Sales Skills Within the Internal Audit Team for Excellence

Sales and relationship skills don't just happen. They're cultivated through shared interests, experience, purpose and reflection. These practical actions show how to make them part of your Internal Audit team's DNA.

Opportunity 1: Focus on the 'How' and Tell or Sell Internal Audit's Journey

Storyteller or checklist completer?

Internal Audit mandates are exactly that in every organization: a set of required standards that apply to every function no matter what. The 'what' is rarely in question, since organizations are governed by a wide range of standards, policies, directives, regulations, and guidelines. But the 'how' is much more qualitative and open to interpretation.

The reality of achieving effective conformance and adding value to the organization requires constant sales and marketing focus, especially on how we go about our work, how we prioritize our views on risks, issues, outcomes, relevance, and value proposition.

Just reflecting on how the Internal Audit team positions itself to sell each of the standard audit deliverables above is a major reality check worth making. Progressive teams will have a clear Vision (and Mission) supported by strategic change initiatives, often grouped into People, Process, Product, and Culture categories. We certainly did, and as we took steps toward our North Star (Vision), we felt proud to share both our change journey and our impact with our stakeholders. It didn't go unnoticed, as we excelled in data analytics, full data audits, and delivered compelling business insights routinely, well before most of our financial services industry peers.

Opportunity 2: Value and Prioritize Informal Opportunities to Connect and Build Relationships with Your Stakeholders and Management

Which aspect of the Internal Audit cycle is more impactful, the formal audit cycle or the informal audit cycle?

Informality builds trust. One senior executive once said to me that I did not come across as an Internal Auditor or Chief Audit Executive: more like a salesman. We were in an informal group catch-up at a Group Leadership offsite meeting in Europe. It was an interesting discussion after a long day, but what piqued his interest was that I was asking forward-looking, open questions about his business and showing genuine interest.

How do they measure success? What risks are out there, and how are they responding to key risks and strategic challenges? What did he think of Internal Audit, and why? How could we ideally help the business?

The above exchange took place as the day was winding down, and we all had a beer or other drink of choice in hand. Informal meetings are often more valuable than scheduled, formal meetings because they lack a fixed agenda. It is critical, though, to know how to ask open questions and to be humble.

Let's be honest, few of us get it right all the time. A key learning opportunity for leaders of Internal Audit teams is to place as much emphasis on relationships and interactions outside of the normal audit cycle as we do on formal meetings. Internal Auditors need to ensure that they are, or are perceived to be, much more than a transactional counterparty by management.

A transactional counterparty is quite restricted to one transaction at a time, and it may be a short-lived interaction. For example, in a securities trading environment, a client may call a salesperson looking for a price to buy USD 20 million of a specific publicly traded bond. The salesperson will offer a price or a price spread for purchases and sales, reflecting parameters agreed with their own trading desk.

If the price is acceptable, they agree to the transaction. If not, there might be some negotiation to strike a deal, but in the end, the buyer may decline based on price and presumably go to a different brokerage house. It is mechanical, routine, and perhaps a bit cold. There is nothing particularly special going on. You take it or leave it.

If we do not take the time and make the effort to build broader, on- and off-audit-cycle relationships with management, there is a risk that Internal Auditors are perceived as just a transactional counterparty. Showing up to perform an audit, no matter how impactful, and then disappearing for years is not a sustainable or valuable approach. Internal Auditors need to become masters of relationship sales, often grounded in shared values, demonstrating care, maintaining informal and formal touchpoints, and building trust.

There are many ways to build that informal connection: coffee, lunch, teach-ins, surveys, sharing quarterly messages, providing insights after each audit, guesting at team meetings, and so on.

For us, quarterly messages covering best practices for broadly relevant topics in our organization were useful three or four times a year to bring to the table for discussion.

These broader messages (typically five to six PowerPoint slides) positioned our Internal Audit team as catalysts for positive organizational change. Management found the 'risk and control' prompts within our insights helpful for their own executive team meetings.

We also generated written insights on almost every audit, providing opportunistic feedback to management on data trends, risks, efficiencies, and culture. Together, these items had a lot of commercial content and built trust among Internal Audit and First Line Management teams.

One analogy I often use is that of the iceberg floating in the ocean. The part of the iceberg above the waterline is akin to the formal audit cycle, it's visible, expected, known, and, if I recall my science studies correctly, typically 10–15% of the iceberg's total mass. This could represent our routine audit work, issues, plans, and reports.

The more interesting part of the iceberg is the part below the waterline; it's not visible, much larger, and requires greater knowledge to navigate safely. Here we have our informal world, where we focus on relationships, generate insights, and learn about and share emerging risk topics. As with the iceberg, the large part below the waterline supports the part above the waterline. It's the same in Internal Audit. Investing in informal touchpoints, sharing insights, and having open risk conversations serves to make our audit issues, reports, and updates more relevant and valuable.

One exercise that can be useful to Internal Audit teams is to reflect broadly on which buckets most of their 'sales and relationship management' activities are taking place in and assess the overall need to rebalance some of these efforts. At a high level, we can think of four main categories:

1. Strategic activities: interactions and updates with your Audit Committee or Chair, the Board, and C-Suite management.
2. Relationship activities: interactions with Internal Audit's key management stakeholders, external audit, and coordinated assurance partners.
3. Execution activities: the routine activities generated by performing internal audits.
4. People or ecosystem activities: best described as team and people activities to develop and maintain Internal Audit risk culture and ensure your department is the place to be.

While there is no magic formula to govern how best to allocate resources to these broad buckets, my suggestion would be to purposely allocate more time to strategic, relationship, and people or ecosystem categories. This will help your team be more impactful. All too often, Internal Audit teams get bogged down in execution mode. Sometimes it's hard to find time to breathe and assess more strategically those subtle, trending changes in the business environment.

Contemplating tough strategic questions and assessing risk scenarios, coupled with high-quality, regular Audit Committee and management interactions, will only help Internal Audit remain relevant by having more of a finger on the pulse. Our people and talent pool are our greatest assets, so it's critical to ensure we have a top-notch operating environment and culture within Internal Audit. We want leadership from every seat, and to do that we must be empowering, fostering open dialogue across all levels in the team, living shared values, failing quickly, and sharing successes together.

I recall and often reference a great piece of advice from a Head of Sales I worked with years ago. His advice to his bond sales force in dealing with large institutional clients was to "always *strive to be number one, but act like you are number two or three.*" What did he mean? He meant be humble, be thankful for the opportunity to trade even if you didn't get the order. Having the right mindset and gratitude for simply being in the game pays dividends as sincere relationships develop.

Opportunity 3: Be Humble, Transparent, and Value Client Input and Feedback

When management and key stakeholders provide candid feedback on Internal Audit, is your glass half-full or half-empty? Can you see or listen to the other side of the argument?

A rock star analogy that comes to mind involves the late, great guitarist Jimi Hendrix. Jimi was asked by a music journalist what it felt like to be the best guitarist in the world.[75] His response was so humble as he looked to take the spotlight away from himself and replied, "*I don't know, you'd have to ask Rory Gallagher.*" Rory was a lesser-known guitarist at the time, but he was also extremely talented. Today, most people would recognize that Jimi Hendrix was the greatest guitarist ever, he had the look, the distorted sound, the hits, and immense ability.

Translated into Internal Audit terms: be humble and don't simply assume that you are always right. Listen to the other side of the argument and share your perspectives and evidence openly. Listen carefully to client feedback, be mindful of how you message potential issues and wordings, and make sure you have an open discussion on any draft observations to validate fact patterns and discuss root causes.

---

75 "Interview with Jimi Hendrix," *Rock & Folk Magazine*, December 1969, reprinted in *Classic Rock Interviews*, ed. Paul Du Noyer (London: Pan Books, 1994).

In my experience, clients don't mind that we find issues in our audits; it is more about how we go about finalizing them and how we word them. If we do find a major issue, then in most cases management will be the first to agree it's important to fix. All too often, Internal Auditors come across as inflexible and unwilling to listen to management feedback, appearing set in their ways and digging in to save face. We all must strive to have an open conversation about the facts and be willing to be flexible if new facts or data emerge that suggest Internal Audit needs to modify or even drop an observation.

Too many times, I have seen Internal Audit teams fail to invest in the ebb and flow of basic human relationships. How many of you have witnessed an unwavering Internal Audit team with one low-rated issue written as if the sky is about to fall, an issue that doesn't even belong in a report to the Board? I certainly have, and it always reflects poorly on Internal Audit.

Invest in listening to client feedback, especially if you are the Chief Audit Executive. We found the adoption of an agile auditing methodology to be helpful here, as our sprint reviews were transparent, and we openly invited management feedback and commentary on observations, risks, and insights. We also arranged client teach-ins before audits to start that listening and feedback cycle.

Opportunity 4: Focus on Key Risk Topics 'Here and Now' and Invest in Continuous Risk Awareness Within Internal Audit

Are you gazing at the stars or your shoes?

Resist the temptation to focus on easier, lower-level risks or less significant audits. This sounds like common sense, but if you want your team to be valued as a strategic asset, you must think strategically and audit the areas that matter to the CEO, Audit Committee, and Executive Management. When audits are being proposed, seek active input from management and your second line and line one and a half colleagues.

Anchor your audit plan to your organization's corporate vision and mission, and your key risk themes, and update these periodically to stay current. If you have a quarterly audit plan, as we did, then market those key risks on your radar for possible subsequent quarters and audits you may be contemplating. Audit Committees love to see a forward-looking view of risk and like to discuss whether they agree or would like to change the focus of future audits. These are always great discussions to have, as they demonstrate our relevance and risk responsiveness.

Networking

The Exponential Power of Good Networking

Developing and maintaining a solid, reliable network is a great personal objective these days, no matter what your profession. Our networks reflect who we are, whom we associate with, what we value, and which industries we belong to. It is an endeavor that helps Internal Auditors perform their independent roles more effectively, builds self-confidence and awareness, and elevates sociability.

A professional network can fulfill many roles: sharing peer ideas, providing support and introductions, mentoring, soliciting feedback, ideation, creativity, or all the above. If you do not focus on your professional and social networking, you are likely not optimizing your capabilities and impact. Building and maintaining an active professional network is a must-do activity, especially for Internal Auditors. I always made a point of keeping in touch with former colleagues, and when I ran my own consultancy a couple of years back, I grew my LinkedIn network dramatically.

Let's be honest, you can't be shy. You never know what new connections might bring in terms of future opportunities for growth or collaboration. So, look to actively build those connections at conferences or by commenting on LinkedIn posts you feel a natural affinity for. Many of my best Internal Audit connections were nurtured via LinkedIn. When you have a point of view that is shared with other reputable Internal Auditors, you find your community.

One great way to gather connections quickly is to post regular thought-provoking polling questions in LinkedIn groups that you are part of; some have hundreds of thousands of members. It was not unusual for my weekly polling questions to receive more than 1,000 responses and thousands more views. That is real marketing. It may feel soft or perhaps a bit strange at first, but it works.

People you follow actively on LinkedIn or other media are posting thought-provoking content daily, and sometimes more than that. It's a hook. Be a bit provocative, and you will find the votes flood in. A byproduct will be an increase in other Internal Auditors checking out your profile and looking to follow you, which of course you can reciprocate.

When you attend an in-person networking event, it is also important to have some objectives going in. Don't just find your friends and have a glass of wine. Try to meet as many new people as you can. Ask for business cards or look to follow up via LinkedIn with at least four or five people you may have met. If you are looking for a new role, let people know.

Most Internal Auditors want to help their community. If you network competently, you may be amazed at what doors can open for you through strangers. Make a strong impression and let your professionalism speak for itself.

Your next role will often come to you from your network, or from your network's networks. If you have 1,000 connections and each of those has 1,000 connections, your sphere of influence in Internal Audit can exceed one million people.[76] You simply never know where your next lead may come from, and you must be proactive in getting out there. If you are between roles, don't sit at home waiting for the phone to ring. That approach belongs to the eighties and nineties mindset, and it will only lead to disappointment.

Make your own luck and be active on LinkedIn and other social media. Write articles, create polls, join networks, and participate in discussions. This is how you put your 'shingle' out there. Join non-profit boards and advisory boards if you can. You may not be paid, but again, the networking and immediate affinity with people who will want to help you will pay large dividends.

Let's be honest, have you ever said no to a friend or former colleague who is looking for help or advice? Of course not. That is one attribute I have witnessed my entire career working in Internal Audit, the power of the Internal Audit global community. It is a very powerful and active force, and with few exceptions, it is a power for good and well worth tapping into.

Case in point: when I was between full-time roles and running my own consultancy, a former colleague introduced me to a partner in a top ten global accounting firm. I had a call with that partner, and we got on well. I was introduced to another partner and had a soft interview for an executive Internal Audit role. Nothing came of it, but we kept in touch. You must remember that failure is a natural outcome but try many times and eventually you will succeed. As the old saying goes, you must cast many lines if you want to be confident of catching a fish.

---

76 LinkedIn Corporation. "Types of LinkedIn Connections." *LinkedIn Help Center*. Accessed November 10, 2025. https://www.linkedin.com/help/linkedin.

The same is true when you are seeking out your next role. A few weeks later, the partner asked if I would participate in an IIA conference panel with them, as they were one of the corporate sponsors. Of course I agreed, as it was to discuss The Future of Internal Audit, a topic I had presented a few months prior to Chartered Accountants Worldwide Network USA, with my former colleague who made the introduction in the first place.

A few months later, we were speaking at the IIA Great Audit Minds (GAM) conference in Texas, one of the biggest global Internal Audit conferences. We had a great time leading a break-out panel discussion before an audience of about 400 people. It was standing room only, and the partner introduced me to several of her colleagues and some senior executives at the IIA.

The partner became a real advocate for me. I was introduced to several companies looking for a new Head of Audit. One role in banking was a good fit, and I actively interviewed for it. I didn't get the role, but I met several great people along the way, senior people that I am now connected with.

A few months later, one of the panelists I had presented with reconnected and purchased online training for his new team, which I was running at the time. While I reentered the full-time workforce soon thereafter, I had networked effectively. Indeed, I continue to introduce colleagues to the accounting firm and to the partner I met, who made the time to get to know me, and vice versa. I am in a position to help them out, given my extensive network of professional accountants. That's how life works these days. While doors are constantly opening and closing, we must make the most of opportunities.

The partner I connected with, and the firm, earned a special place in my heart. They really tried to help me when I needed their help, and these days, I make a point to reciprocate opportunities and introduce talented professionals to them. I never worked there, but I feel an affinity for this organization, given the positive impression they made on me when I was actively networking for my next role.

What You Put into It Is What You Get Out of It

For internal auditors, effective networking is a lot more than simply collecting contacts. It's about cultivating credibility and selling your brand. What you put into it is exactly what you'll get back, multiplied through trust and reputation.

I have always strived to maintain a decent network, keeping in touch with colleagues and expanding my sphere of influence and influencers. Social media makes this so much easier than in the old days.

During the early part of the global pandemic, I noticed a Chartered Accountants Worldwide Network post looking for new volunteer board members in the US. It piqued my interest because I am a Chartered Accountant and had actively participated in its predecessor organization back in the mid-nineties. I was impressed by the organization's website and conference recap.

Soon, I applied for a volunteer board role and looked forward to giving back to the US-based Chartered Accountants community, drawing on my career experience on Wall Street and with a global insurer. A few interviews later, I found myself as a volunteer Board Member. Roll forward a few years, and I am now President of the Board (a volunteer position) and actively involved in leading and developing various strategic, educational, and networking activities supporting a network of Chartered Accountants in the US, Canada, and the Caribbean.

While I have actively given back to my peers through this network, I have learned so much from my fellow Board and network members, developing new skills and interests along the way. Volunteering is a great way to build advocacy. Shared interests typically breed close relationships and trust, and these relationships can open endless doors for you in your professional career.

When you have been on a board of directors with someone for a couple of years, you build a close relationship, an affinity, and a sense of shared purpose. I always speak highly of my volunteer colleagues, as I know they have made sacrifices and done all the right things when nobody was looking. Such integrity and selflessness deserve recognition and advocacy, and I am sure many leaders feel the same. So, seize volunteer, non-profit, and advisory board opportunities and broaden your professional horizons.

Internal Advocates

How much time do you devote to identifying and connecting with internal advocates for your cause? Many people, including internal auditors, assume someone has their back, can pitch their name in the ring for new opportunities etc. Reality is, we must actively cultivate our advocacy network by being present, known for great work and having a voice of reason that is listened to and heard. In any corporation, it is critical to have people who advocate for you both informally and formally, people who know you and believe in your ability to add value, be fair and objective, and act progressively. Devoting time to identifying and solidifying your internal advocates is a critical endeavor.

I can recall many times when we were looking to fill a role that had opened in our Internal Audit team, and the shortlist of internal candidates was quickly assembled through their advocacy network. Advocates are trusted and know when to put your name forward and how to best position you for consideration.

Opinions of advocates are respected and taken seriously, and they are often guiding organizational hands that operate largely behind the scenes. Your advocates should be individuals you know well and have a strong rapport with. Sometimes it will be a peer, a manager in your own department, or someone working within another assurance function. Better yet, it could be a key client relationship.

Be perceived by your clients as adding value to their business through issues, insights, and shared calls to action, and you will find that great opportunities will come your way. For Internal Auditors, key advocates could be external to your team. For example, external audit management who have worked closely with you, or a Board Member or Audit Committee Chair with whom you have built a strong rapport. So, allocate time to identifying and nurturing a few key advocates, and let them know how and when they may be able to help you. Be transparent about your personal growth and career ambitions.

One challenge that Internal Auditors often face when presented with a great new opportunity outside their current team is that they don't want to leave Internal Audit. As we say back home, "Don't look a gift horse in the mouth." Roles outside of Internal Audit can be great ways to further your assurance capabilities and broaden your business acumen and relationship skills.

For me, the eight-plus years I spent working outside Internal Audit only served to mold me into a much better auditor. I ultimately transitioned back into a more senior Internal Audit management role with an arsenal of new skills that set me apart. Sometimes, in your career, taking a challenging role outside of Internal Audit could be the best move you ever make in terms of boosting your assurance and managerial skill sets. It worked out just fine for me following strategy and client relationship roles, and I openly recommend others to be open to such possibilities rather than being blinkered by the comfort of staying in Internal Audit.

Indeed, staying too long in one Internal Audit team and not experiencing corporate life on the other side of the fence can be a detrimental career decision. If you lack ambition, drive, or a desire for new learning and skills, you may slowly lose relevance and impact. This is especially true these days, given the speed of risk evolution and the emergence of AI-driven assurance.

Being an advocate for others who are talented and demonstrate real impact and value is equally important. I took pride in being an active advocate for people in my team and beyond. Being a source of encouragement and soft recommendations can be very fulfilling, especially when you see people moving into new roles and adding great value, demonstrating that your trust and belief in them were well placed. As an advocate, you know they are capable, and your support may just provide the extra push they need.

Getting to Know People

Ask yourself: How much time do you currently spend on relationship-building versus audit execution? What informal opportunities exist in your organization to build trust and visibility? Reflecting on questions like these will really help you jump start your approach to building a better, more visible personal brand. It is human nature to gravitate toward people we know and trust. Think about it: you could probably say some outrageous things to your best friend, and regardless of whether you are serious or joking, they will either agree, push back, or laugh it off. They trust you no matter what their gut reaction.

Another example: if you find yourself attending a large industry conference and in the plenary session you spot someone you know, you will most likely find yourself stopping by to say hello. Why? Because you feel comfortable with them. It's a lot harder to strike up a meaningful conversation with attendees you don't know. To be a great Internal Auditor, you must invest time in getting to know people.

One of the great skills of an Internal Auditor is not always knowing the answer but knowing who to ask to get it. That may sound counterintuitive, but it clearly demonstrates the power of good networking. So, make the time to be genuinely interested in your peers and colleagues. Coffee catchups, lunches, and corporate social activities are all great ways to get to know people. We can gain tremendous business knowledge and context on the current business environment and conditions through proactive and informal conversations with management.

Internal Audit teams should hold teach-ins for other teams outside of the formal audit cycle to share perspectives on good risk management and assurance practices. Some of the best times we had were our periodic team dinners when we invited a few members from management or other assurance functions. Nothing fancy, it was often a curry house in the UK, but the food and company were great. Impactful internal auditing is about people, earning their trust, understanding their goals, and helping them succeed. The stronger your relationships, the greater your impact. And what better way to build strong relationships than connecting over an Indian meal with some management colleagues? Ah, I miss the great times we had dining at the Shifnal Balti!

Recap of Key Learnings in this Chapter:

1. Invest in developing your sales and relationship management skills to become a more differentiated, effective Internal Audit leader.

2. Be much more than a transactional sales counterparty. Recognize the need to focus on and flex your style to master strategic sales, relationship sales, and how to market your function as the place for talent and leadership development.

3. Strike a balance between strategic, relationship, and people sales activities versus pure audit execution sales activities. Devoting more time to the former will enhance the quality of your audits through increased strategic relevance, risk responsiveness, and an empowered team with leadership from every seat.

4. Leverage the informal audit cycle as much as the formal audit cycle. Remember, just like an iceberg, the informal audit cycle is akin to the part of the iceberg below the waterline, it is far larger and more impactful to the overall value perception of your Internal Audit team than the formal audit process. Performing good audits is essential, but so is nurturing relationships, communica-

Recap of Key Learnings in this Chapter:

tion, and insight. Remember the iconic musical examples born from informality: A Flock of Seagulls' haircut, Motörhead's trailblazing double bass drumbeat, and Ronnie James Dio's maloik!

5. Develop and maintain a strong network of both internal and external advocates. Meeting new people, sharing your story, and finding common ground will keep your network vibrant.

6. Don't wait until you are in dire need of help to find a new role. Build out your network every day, and you will find that many professionals know you and will advocate for you. The bigger and wider your social media network is, the better. You never know where your next opportunity may come from, so maintain an active social media presence and engaging commentary to keep your network alive and thriving.

Chapter 15

INTERNAL AUDITS FUTURE - AUGMENTED ASSURANCE REFLECTING OUR HUMAN COMPETENCIES AND AI

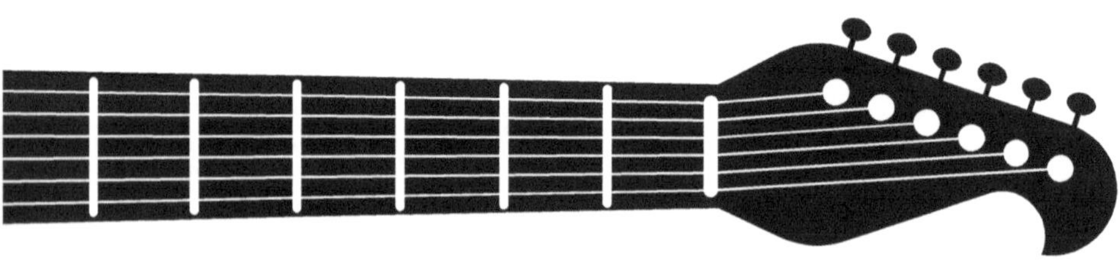

Survival of the fittest, or the most adaptable?

I believe strongly in the future of Internal Audit. We have a very bright future if we embrace data and technology skill sets and leverage artificial intelligence tools, to accentuate our human capabilities. We must ditch some of the historical practices and ways of thinking that don't differentiate our work or add value to today's digital world.

According to history, Neanderthals went extinct for a reason: they could not adapt to their environment. Maybe they wanted to, but they couldn't, and unfortunately, they didn't.

Fast forward to 2026, internal auditors face a similar challenge. Our choice is between innovating, adapting technology and AI tools to accentuate our core human values, or sticking to our traditional playbook and fading away into the sunset. I know which path appeals to me. With the advent of artificial intelligence, we are at a strategic crossroads, and much earlier than many of us in the profession would have guessed. AI is changing everything that we do, and quickly.

If you think about the Internal Audit profession in two big buckets of activity, the What and the How, the impact of AI will be immense.

Delivery of our 'WHAT' can now be supercharged. Deploying AI tools and agents is like having 100 staff at your disposal. Your prompts for guidance on aspects of risk, controls, behaviors, etc. can yield immediate and valuable output. Of course, we will still need to own this output, review it, adjust it where necessary and deliver the key messages around it.

With AI on our side, we have no more excuses. AI can give us answers, and good ones, to almost any question we have on risk and internal controls coverage by Internal Audit.

Internal Audit's Great Leap Forward

Future assurance will be almost real-time, with AI-driven large language models assessing control outcomes as they occur. Large, well-capitalized firms will adopt this technology first, while other firms will face some inertia as their organizations and management resist the extent of AI-driven assurance models in the short to medium term.

Trust is a key concept in deploying AI tools and models. Yes, many of us already believe that the possibilities are endless, but do we trust the outcomes or the speed of delivery? For many, the speed of change delivery feels a bit suspicious. That's probably not a surprise, as we are human, and we are the constraining factor in AI adoption. Regulators may be in a similar boat. One can imagine a future where there are many AI regulations to comply with, and perhaps some areas where AI deployment is either not allowed or limited by law.

There will be many different viewpoints across our profession, however, the genie is already out of the bottle. With AI, we must pivot from being historic reporters to being forward-looking risk and control challengers and adverse outcome predictors. Over time, business activities will be processed via well-designed and continuously improving AI/large language models. Real value will come from the logic and risk scenarios these models may miss or simply have not yet considered. This is where Internal Audit and human intellect can generate more forward-looking impact and insights.

So, every Internal Audit team and other assurance function, should by now be experimenting with AI prompting and using it to make their assurance work and reports higher quality and more productive. AI enablement should form part of every Internal Audit Team's Vision.

The 'HOW' may also be impacted and enabled by AI, as we can seek real-time guidance on best practices. However, I believe the 'HOW' will remain the real human element and differentiator: how we as people interact with each other, value each other, message, and resonate. No AI algorithm is going to replace poor delivery or poor messaging around Internal Audit activities, issues or stakeholder interactions. That responsibility will remain a human endeavor.

Transparency around messaging audit results will remain critical, but we should all expect the delivery speed to accelerate significantly. Ninety-day audits may soon feel like relics from the Stone Age. AI should help us craft our messages and deliver them much closer to real time. More likely days and weeks, rather than months.

Another benefit of this great leap forward will be our ability to cover more of the risk universe, but we should also expect the risk universe itself to expand and change more quickly, reflecting increased complexity derived from both the speed of AI adoption and exponential growth expected in AI use cases. A new risk management paradigm will emerge, and we will need to harden responsible AI to keep up.

Change will be our only constant.

Punk Rocker Gary Numan Discovers a Mini Moog and Shapes the Sound of Eighties Synthesizer Pop Music

Back in the late seventies, Gary Numan, an aspiring punk rocker, went into the recording studio with his band Tubeway Army. Fully expecting to record a punk-oriented album, he noticed some electronic gear stashed in the corner of the recording studio as his bandmates unloaded their van of equipment. It was a Mini Moog[77], an early analog synthesizer.

Numan turned the Mini Moog on and was immediately mesmerized by the depth of its sound and clean notes, which he experimented with and layered for effect. The entire studio shook when he played it, and he raved that he had tried, but could never get such sound and effect from his guitar. That sound proved to be a game-changer, so much so that Gary and Tubeway Army decided to take a totally different musical path. They changed their original plans to record a punk album and sought to leverage the Mini Moog into their recording sessions and songs, forging a synthesizer sound. They chose to innovate rather than

77 Numan, Gary. Interview by The Vinyl Guide Podcast. *The Gary Numan Interview – The Vinyl Guide Podcast, Episode 284*. YouTube video, discussing the Minimoog story in the last chapter. Published on YouTube: https://www.youtube.com/watch?v=PGsoEQqbRhgg

imitate. It was a tough pivot, and they had to be doggedly determined to alter the course with their record company. A real lesson in inner toughness.

The predecessor Moog was the staple of early seventies rock bands like Emerson, Lake and Palmer and Deep Purple. They produced great organ sounds but literally required a 40-foot container truck of equipment to connect the circuits. It was great for big rock bands playing on the world stage, but simply not practical for new entrants driving their own van across the UK!

Not only did Gary master the instrument and sound, but he emerged as one of the very early 'Godfathers' of the synthesizer sound. While Gary and Tubeway Army were not the first synthesizer band (Kraftwerk and Ultravox typically are recognized as being among the first such bands), they were among the most impactful and recognizable for their sound and found massive chart success in the late seventies and early eighties.

Synthesizers are often described as the sound that defined the early eighties New Wave of music. Indeed, Gary and Tubeway Army recorded their global hit song *Are 'Friends' Electric?*[78] in 1979, well before A Flock of Seagulls or The Human League hits became mainstream.

Tubeway Army adapted technology and literally helped to create a new genre of music: Synthesizer Pop. While other electronic bands were already out there for a couple of years, Tubeway Army were the first electronic music band to achieve a number one song. Other huge hits followed, such as Cars,[79] a radio station staple to this day. Despite these songs being over forty years old, many would freely admit they set an incredibly high bar for a new genre of music at the time.

---

78 Numan, Gary. *"Are 'Friends' Electric?"* Performed by Tubeway Army. Written by Gary Numan. Released May 1979. Beggars Banquet Records.

79 *Cars* written and produced by Gary Numan and performed by Gary Numan and his band. The song was released on August 24, 1979 and issued by the Beggars Banquet record label.

So, what can Internal Auditors Learn from Gary Numan and Tubeway Army?

Change is the only constant, and if we want to be relevant, we must adapt our technology and approach to auditing. We must innovate. The onset and application of AI is our 'Mini Moog moment,' and we must embrace this change and set forth a new Internal Audit genre, beyond traditional or even agile auditing. Real-time assurance beckons.

Hidden in Gary's music is a certain and accepted simplicity. He freely admits that he, at the time, was an average guitarist and musician. However, his creativity, curiosity, and playing style (simple riffs, long notes, and layered sound) make his music so appealing to the masses.

Similarly, we must remember as Internal Auditors that our efforts will not amount to much if we fail to communicate clearly with intent and add value to our management and board stakeholders. Our human characteristics will always be at the forefront of how we as internal auditors deliver value.

The Future of Internal Audit Requires Balancing our Human Behavioral Competencies and Technology Skill Sets

Every Internal Audit department operates differently, and there is a broad spectrum of Internal Audit functions out there. If your Internal Audit future is not focused on mastering skill sets in areas such as data analytics and the understanding and application of artificial intelligence, then you will increasingly find it difficult to be differentiated and to add value to the business.

Internal Auditors may be risking extinction if they fail to adapt in the short to medium term. Exactly how much time is anyone's guess, but the clock is most certainly ticking.

Independence, integrity, and objectivity will remain at our core, however, it is our value orientation and ability to adapt at speed that will keep Internal Auditors relevant.

We can add value by bringing the human elements more clearly into focus (empathy, creativity, curiosity, honesty, courage, clarity, etc.) being differentiated through demonstration of data and technology savviness and delivering more forward-looking issues and insights to help the business thrive in a digital and data-centric world.

The expectations placed on Internal Audit by our stakeholders and management continue to increase and have never been higher. So, where does Internal Audit go from here, and what is our future? Just like Spinal Tap, our internal audit amplifiers now need to go to eleven.

Internal Audit finds itself again at a strategic crossroads in its evolution, and the changes driven by artificial intelligence and digitalization are driving innovation and strategic repositioning. Let us not forget the emergence of information technology audits a few decades ago. Back then, everything was going to change. Technology was going to change the face of Internal Audit forever.

It did, for sure. Look how well Internal Auditors leverage technology these days. Data science capabilities and cutting-edge technology often form core skill sets within Internal Audit. Information technology did not replace Internal Auditors; it just made us more useful and capable.

Artificial or Augmented Intelligence?

Today, we may pose similar questions about the impact of artificial intelligence on Internal Audit. Artificial intelligence will reshape Internal Audit and many corporate functions as we know them today, and there will be a transformation of what we do and how we do it. A new set of norms will emerge and, no doubt, new productivity gains and efficiencies. All of us in Internal Audit roles should be asking ourselves whether artificial intelligence is a tsunami or perhaps a surfer's dream wave. I believe that AI will augment our core capabilities and proficiencies rather than replacing them.

Internal Auditors have never been more relevant and valued than they are today. To sustain our value, we must be ready for all eventualities. While none of us has a crystal ball, if change is our only constant, then key areas where we should anticipate Internal Audit change in the short to medium term include:

1 – Expansion of the Core Competencies that define the role of Internal Auditors

It used to be that most Internal Auditors had a background in accounting and finance, me included. The speed of business was much slower, technology was emerging, and if you were like me in a Big Eight firm in the early nineties, your choice of specialty was Audit, Tax, or Management Consulting. The business environment was not as complicated or as technology enabled as it is today.

We have witnessed an explosion in business complexity in the past decade, and the space of growth continues. Indeed, the global pandemic only seemed to spur even faster digitalization, as we all found ourselves homebound as workers and consumers. The emergence of scalable and affordable artificial intelligence in the last couple of years will dramatically impact how Internal Audit capabilities evolve.

Today, there are far more specialist areas within the corporate world, and these continue to mushroom with new technology, including artificial intelligence. So today we all speak about cyber risks, data science integration, blockchain adoption, decarbonization, and robotic processing, including the unique risks and opportunities that stem from these technologies.

Internal Auditors must continue to invest in both their core skills and new emerging skills sets to maintain relevance. This is true no matter the size of the Internal Audit team. Maintaining a continuous learning and improvement mindset will help auditors keep progressing.

Failing to invest in critical new skill sets would risk our relevance, and the pace of change will not allow much room to rest on our laurels.

Being data and tech-savvy is a must. Keeping on top of best practices is time well spent. A silver lining is that with all the new risks to assess, having a diverse pool of skills and competencies within the audit team will be a real advantage.

2 – Shortening of Assurance Delivery Cycles

Traditional auditing is largely sample-based assurance. We test a sample and find a couple of anomalies, then infer from statistics that there are issues with outcomes and internal controls. In many Internal Audit functions, audits still take three to four months to conclude end-to-end.

Today, with digitization, we can perform data-driven audits covering full populations of transactions. But our delivery speed can still be a challenge. I was a Chief Audit Executive in a global financial services firm, and almost all our audits were of full populations and data-driven, even pre-pandemic. Our delivery time using agile auditing was still roughly 60 to 90 days and sometimes longer than that.

However, the level of assurance from a data-driven audit is much greater than from a traditional audit, as you are testing all transactions and sizing actual outliers and anomalies more precisely. These differences enhance assurance, making data-driven audits significantly more valuable.

As a profession, how can we improve our delivery to achieve warp speed? We should AI-enable Internal Audit's data prowess and our ability to interrogate and change data hypotheses more in real time, ideally with management working alongside us.

Whether AI-enabled or not, the future of Internal Audit may resemble a conference call with management to view and adjust hypotheses in real time, leveraging AI prompts and discussing the results as they appear. Augmented intelligence on display.

My expectation is that audit cycles will shorten dramatically as our auditing methodologies are infused with AI. Near real-time audits and assurance through AI are a real possibility for some large tech organizations. The stuff we used to dream of is now almost in reach.

3 – Blurring or elimination of boundaries between the lines of defense

Most moderate to large-sized organizations will have several assurance functions working alongside each other, each with a different mandate to provide value to key Board stakeholders and shareholders. Taken together, we serve to help make our organizations thrive: taking informed risk decisions, being compliant with rules and regulations, achieving good outcomes for customers, and ensuring the organization has effective standards, policies, and internal controls.

Digitization has reinforced the notion that data is the lifeblood of any organization. If you take a step back from the various assurance activities, you will see that most assurance work is devoted to gathering, assessing, and reporting on datasets and data pools, and assessing data conformance with corporate standards, policies, procedures, and regulations.

While the assurance mandates of each assurance function may all be different, increasing the core capability in handling and analyzing large data pools may well make a compelling case for integration among today's separate assurance teams. Having strong data science skills sets and investing in AI know-how across the Internal Audit team will help position Internal Audit for the future.

An internal 'war' for AI and data analytics skills is coming, and differentiation in this space will help Internal Auditors preserve their relevance.

Critical capabilities include accessing full datasets, ensuring the data is normalized, running data hypotheses, handling exceptions and false positives, sizing anomalies, and assessing root causes of any poor outcomes.

Add artificial intelligence into the mix, and all bets regarding the necessity to maintain separate Line 1.5, 2, and Line 3 functions in any organization blur. While historic well-established governance norms will persist for now, don't be surprised if a leaner organizational governance model emerges. We should all expect the unexpected.

The assurance team that becomes a deft hand in using AI-enabled prompts and agents to deliver greater organizational value in real time will hold the high ground in this battle. Organizations are already examining the overlaps across the historic

Lines of Defense and the opportunity for productivity gains and further integration.

Don't be a passive observer. Tune in and aim to set a blazing pace in AI adoption within your organization. When it comes to AI use and the corporate value proposition, Internal Auditors must be perceived as the car driver, not a passive passenger, or worse, someone outside chasing the vehicle down the road!

4 – Will the Co-Sourcing Model continue to grow, or contract with AI adoption in Internal Audit?

Unless you are part of a large Internal Audit team, let's say fifty plus people. It is very difficult to have every skill set in-house required to perform great, relevant audits for your organization. Add to that the increasing speed of new technologies and emerging risks, and it will only become more challenging to operate a full-service Internal Audit team. That may be where AI-enablement comes in and perhaps offers up a self-directed alternative to Internal Audit co-sourcing. That said, I would expect that professional co-sourcing providers are investing heavily in their own AI capabilities and will offer 'AI auditing as a service' via AI bots and agents, to their clients.

One certainty is that new skills will be required by Internal Audit teams to cover new and emerging risks that matter to their organizations.

Audit Committees and Boards may increasingly recognize that external resources will likely become a permanent part of Internal Audit. Many Internal Audit teams operate co-sourcing models today, so that aspect is not new, but it is likely that the breadth of change across our industry will be the true shift.

As is often the case with technological change, it may be cheaper in the long run to buy in expertise from third parties, rather than trying to replicate those capabilities in-house.

5 – AI, Our Greatest Opportunity or Greatest Threat?

The pessimist in me can see AI adoption contributing to increased risk of bias, data privacy breaches, and fraud. Dark side risks persist with AI and internal auditors must remain as leading voices for responsible AI governance, transparency, and oversight. These broader societal and organizational challenges will be sources of renewed Internal Audit opportunities. Could we see AI go rogue? What safeguards will organizations deploying artificial intelligence require? Who will assess and monitor deployment practices and controls? Which function is trusted to assess the complexity of AI governance and standards conformance?

While there has been lots of myopic speculation about the impact of artificial intelligence on the role and relevance of Internal Audit teams, I believe opportunities will continue to abound for us.

So, let's avoid the temptation to be written off by others, quite so quickly. Our executive stakeholders will look to Internal Audit because we are trusted, apply critical thinking and can communicate succinctly. While AI tools are by no means perfect yet and do sometimes offer up a 'three-legged chicken' as their hallucinated truth, AI offers some out-of-the-box use cases for Internal Audit. They can be excellent real-time audit planning assistants and offer wording suggestions for issues and reports, data analysis and presentation, and we can train AI models to assess policy and standards conformance across vast datasets.

The human elements and dynamics will become more important and critical linchpins, underscoring our artificial intelligence journey. Within our organizations, Internal Audit will help to ensure valid risk-taking and good outcomes are being achieved without bias. The role of Internal Audit will change, but it will always require a strong human element to be fully effective.

Applying expert judgment, assessing outcomes, challenging the status quo, reporting objectively, and communicating results clearly will always be competencies in high demand. As Internal Audit leaders, we must continue to lead by demonstrating core human capabilities, while finding inspiration from our many real rockstar examples. Let's recap some of our shared core competencies that will help all of us take it to the next level, our eleven, a la Spinal Tap:

Resilience (Foghat)

Honesty and Asking for Feedback (Lemmy Kilmister)

Agility and Continuous Learning (Ronnie Van Zant and Lynyrd Skynyrd)

Integrity and Finding our True Voice (Rory Gallagher)

Courage to speak up (John Lydon) and Empathy (John Lydon / The Sex Pistols)

Creativity and Vision (David Bowie)

Connecting with our audience (Albert Collins, Freddie Mercury)

Humbleness (Jimi Hendrix)

Leadership and being candid (Bob Geldof)

Marketing leadership (KISS)

Spontaneity (A Flock of Seagulls)

Listening to and Actioning Feedback (Phil Taylor / Motörhead)

Being Yourself (Ronnie James Dio)

Curiosity, Adaptability and Innovation (Gary Numan and Tubeway Army)

Communicating with confidence, demonstrating our objectivity and courage, and using our collective voices to influence better outcomes for our organizations will never go old. Equally, we must ensure data savviness and technology skills become core components of our Internal Audit DNA so we can excel in adding value to our organizations, as artificial intelligence tools become mainstream.

So, learn from ancient history and don't miss this boat. Innovate and adapt continuously. Invest in your core human behavioral and leadership competencies to be an Internal Audit Rockstar. Continually adapt your data, technology, and AI skill sets now to augment and position your Internal Audit team, and yourself, for the future. Do not go extinct like the Neanderthals.

Change is our only constant.

Recap of Key Learnings in this Chapter:

1. Adapt your skill sets and competencies continuously or face extinction.

2. Great things can come from technological adaptation however, the human element will always be critical to our success. We must embrace change just like Gary Numan and Tubeway Army did back in 1979, when they forged a new synthesizer music sound for the masses. Despite AI-driven changes in Internal Audit approaches and coverage, we must always own the need for clear, valued communication of impact, outcomes, and opportunities with our management and board stakeholders. The human element will remain critical and differentiating for internal auditors.

3. Embrace technological change in Internal Audit. Invest in mastering artificial intelligence usage and prompting, and other emerging technologies, to boost your productivity, delivery speed, and the value of your 'WHAT.'

4. Focus your efforts on differentiating your 'HOW' to sharpen your value delivery and human behavioral competencies.

Recap of Key Learnings in this Chapter:

5. Be ready for massive and fast-paced change in assurance delivery as AI speeds up digital business models and automates assurance.

6. Internal Audit delivery timeframes will shorten dramatically. Expect consolidation of previously separate assurance functions and activities spanning Lines of Defense 1.5 (Business Governance teams), 2 (Risk Management and Compliance teams), and 3 (Internal Audit teams).

7. Don't become complacent. Artificial intelligence tools will spur a great leap forward for Internal Audit teams, with Internal Audit likely playing a corporate oversight role over ethical and fair AI deployment and business cases. Seize these opportunities fully and without hesitation.

Credits & Acknowledgements

1. Chambers, Richard F. Trusted Advisors: Key Attributes of Outstanding Internal Auditors, 2nd ed. Hoboken, NJ: Wiley, 2019.

2. *This is Spinal Tap* – 1984 mockumentary film written by Christopher Guest, Michael McKean, Harry Shearer and Rob Reiner.

3. 'Celtic Tiger' – a nickname for Ireland during its boom years between 1995 and 2007 when the Irish economy was growing rapidly. The Irish economy grew at an average annual rate of 9.4% between 1995 and 2000.

4. Foghat *Slow Ride* – released by Bearsville records in 1975, written by Dave Peverett, produced by Nick Jameson.

5. Joe Miller, Defender of the Faith, "Roger Earl (Foghat) Interview," November 17, 2023 https://defendersofthefaithmetal.com/roger-earl-foghat-interview/

6. Joe Miller, Defender of the Faith, "Roger Earl (Foghat) Interview," November 17, 2023 https://defendersofthefaithmetal.com/roger-earl-foghat-interview/

7. *Foghat, A Blues Tribute* – recorded in New York City at the Palladium Theatre in 1977 as a benefit concert to save the blues record collection at The New York Public Library. Performers included: Foghat, Eddie 'Bluesman' Kirkland, John Lee Hooker, Muddy Waters, Paul Butterfield, Johnny Winter, Otis Blackwell, Dave 'Honeyboy' Edwards.

8. *Lemmy the Movie* – A documentary film which celebrates the life and rock 'n' roll philosophy of Motörhead frontman and bassist Lemmy. Directed by Wes Orshoski and Greg Oliver, released on January 13, 2011, and distributed by Lionsgate Canada.

9. *The Accountant*, released in 2016, written by Bill Dubuque, directed by Gavin O'Connor and starring Ben Affleck.

10. 'Ultra Vires' is a Latin phrase meaning beyond the powers. In legal terms it means any action by a company or its agents that exceeds the legal scope of its authority.

11. Audit tick marks are symbols or notations used by auditors during the audit process to document their work and to denote auditing actions taken during testing or review activities.

12. *Motörhead: Live Fast Die Old* documentary, 2005, directed by Alex Berk, with Miranda Sawyer, Lemmy Kilmister, Phil Campbell and Mikkey Dee.

13. Gallup, State of the Global Workplace 2023 Report (Washington, D.C.: Gallup Press, 2023), https://www.gallup.com/workplace/349484/state-of-the-global-workplace.aspx

14. Rolling Stone. *Inside the Lynyrd Skynyrd Plane Crash That Killed Ronnie Van Zant, Steve Gaines and Cassie Gaines.* Rolling Stone, October 20, 2022 https://www.rollingstone.com/music/music-features/lynyrd-skynyrd-plane-crash-1977-ronnie-van-zant-1234618710/

15. *If I Leave Here Tomorrow: A Film About Lynyrd Skynyrd*, directed by Stephen Kijak (Los Angeles: CMT / Passion Pictures, 2018).

16. Markman, Ron. *Lynyrd Skynyrd: Remembering the Free Birds of Southern Rock.* New York: HarperCollins, 2006.

17. *ChatGPT* is a generative artificial intelligence chatbot developed by OpenAI and launched in 2022.

18. Ries, Eric. *The Lean Startup: How Today's Entrepreneurs Use Continuous Innovation to Create Radically Successful Businesses.* New York: Crown Business, 2011.

19. BBC Archives. Interview with John Lydon (BBC Radio 1, 1978). Originally recorded in 1978, first aired in 2013. London: British Broadcasting Corporation.

20. Dame Janet Smith. *The Dame Janet Smith Review: Report of the Investigation into Matters Relating to Jimmy Savile at the BBC.* London: British Broadcasting Corporation, 2016.

21. Securities and Exchange Commission (U.S.). *Rule 15c3-3, Customer Protection – Reserves and Custody of Securities.* Code of Federal Regulations, Title 17, §240.15c3-3. Washington, DC: Government Publishing Office, current through 2025.

22. Muise, Dan. *Gallagher, Marriott, Derringer, and Trower: Their Lives and Music.* Bloomington, IN: iUniverse, 2002.

23. *Ghost Blues: The Story of Rory Gallagher,* a documentary film directed by Ian Thuiller and released by Capo Records on September 14, 2010. Directed by Ian Thullier. London: Eagle Vision, 2010. The film explores the life and musical journey of Rory Gallagher and includes reflections from many musicians and commentators who knew him well.

24. Rick Beato. 2025. "Aerosmith's Joe Perry and Brad Whitford Talk about Rory Gallagher." *YouTube short,* January 2, 2025. https://www.youtube.com/shorts/NqLLyXy9BOw.

25. *Official UK Singles Chart archive (NME/BPI historical notes).*

26. BBC. *Sex Pistols – Huddersfield Christmas Day Concert Footage* (archival film, 1977). London: British Broadcasting Corporation.

27. World Economic Forum. *The Global Risks Report 2024.* Geneva: World Economic Forum, 2024.

28. Taleb, Nassim Nicholas. *The Black Swan: The Impact of the Highly Improbable.* New York: Random House, 2007.

29. McKinsey & Company. *The State of AI 2024: Generative AI's Next Frontier.* McKinsey Global Institute, 2024.

30. Edwards, A. Murphy. Quoted in Lloyd Mallan, *Men, Rockets, and Space Rats.* New York: Random House, 1957.

31. International Monetary Fund. *World Economic Outlook: Globalization in Transition*. Washington, DC: IMF, 2023.

32. World Economic Forum. *The Global Risks Report 2024*. Geneva: World Economic Forum, 2024.

33. Beck, Kent, et al. *Manifesto for Agile Software Development.* Agile Alliance, 2001. https://agilemanifesto.org/

34. Shakespeare, William. *Macbeth.* Edited by Barbara A. Mowat and Paul Werstine. New York: Simon & Schuster, 2003.

35. Atlassian. *Jira Software.* Accessed November 2025. https://www.atlassian.com/software/jira

36. Schwaber, Ken, and Jeff Sutherland. *The Scrum Guide: The Definitive Guide to Scrum: The Rules of the Game.* Scrum.org, November 2020.

37. Basel Committee on Banking Supervision. International Convergence of Capital Measurement and Capital Standards: A Revised Framework. Basel, Switzerland: Bank for International Settlements, 2006.

38. Institute of Internal Auditors. *The IIA's Three Lines Model: An Update of the Three Lines of Defense.* Lake Mary, FL: The Institute of Internal Auditors, 2020.

39. Committee of Sponsoring Organizations of the Treadway Commission (COSO). *Internal Control—Integrated Framework.* Durham, NC: COSO, 2013.

40. Financial Conduct Authority. *FG21/5: The FCA's Approach to Supervision of Internal Audit and Assurance Functions.* London: Financial Conduct Authority, 2021.

41. Institute of Internal Auditors (IIA). *The IIA Global Internal Audit Competency Framework.* (Lake Mary, FL: The Institute of Internal Auditors, 2020).

42. Tichy, Noel M., and Stratford Sherman. *Control Your Destiny or Someone Else Will: How Jack Welch Is Making General Electric the World's Most Competitive Company.* New York: Doubleday, 1993.

43. Robert K. Greenleaf, *Servant Leadership: A Journey into the Nature of Legitimate Power and Greatness* (New York: Paulist Press, 1977).

44. David Leaf and Ken Sharp, *KISS: Behind the Mask—The Official Authorized Biography* (New York: Warner Books, 2003).

45. Lynyrd Skynyrd, *Freebird*, recorded 1973, on *Pronounced 'Lĕh-'nérd 'Skin-'nérd*, MCA Records, 1973.

46. The Ramones, *Blitzkrieg Bop*, recorded 1976, on *Ramones*, Sire Records, 1976.

47. Rolling Stone. "The 100 Greatest Singers of All Time." *Rolling Stone*, updated January 2023. https://www.rollingstone.com/music/music-lists/100-greatest-singers-of-all-time-147019/

48. Humble Pie, *Thirty Days in the Hole*, recorded 1972, on *Smokin'*, A&M Records, 1972.

49. Black Sabbath, *Neon Knights*, recorded 1980, on *Heaven and Hell*, Vertigo Records, 1980.

50. Scorpions, *Rock You Like a Hurricane*, recorded 1984, on *Love at First Sting*, Harvest/EMI Records, 1984.

51. Beck, Kent et al. *Manifesto for Agile Software Development*. Agile Alliance, 2001. https://agilemanifesto.org/.

52. McKinsey & Company. *The State of AI in 2024: Accelerating Change and Transformation.* New York: McKinsey Global Institute, 2024.

53. The Institute of Internal Auditors. *International Standards for the Professional Practice of Internal Auditing (Standards).* Lake Mary, FL: The Institute of Internal Auditors, 2017.

54. Schwaber, Ken, and Jeff Sutherland. *The Scrum Guide: The Definitive Guide to Scrum: The Rules of the Game.* Scrum.org, 2020.

55. Austin, Robert D. *Measuring and Managing Performance in Organizations.* New York: Dorset House Publishing, 1996.

56. OpenAI. *ChatGPT (GPT-4) Technical Report.* San Francisco: OpenAI, 2023. https://arxiv.org/abs/2303.08774.

57. The Boomtown Rats, *I Don't Like Mondays*, track 1 on *The Fine Art of Surfacing*, Ensign Records, 1979.

58. Live Aid. "Bob Geldof Urges Donations." Broadcast July 13, 1985. BBC Television, London.

59. BBC News. "Live Aid: The Day the Music Changed the World." July 13, 2015. https://www.bbc.com/news/entertainment-arts-33476380.

60. The London Gazette. "Honorary Knighthood Conferred upon Bob Geldof." January 1986.

61. The Guardian. "Bob Geldof: From Punk Rocker to Humanitarian." July 12, 2020. https://www.theguardian.com/music.

62. BBC Newsnight. "David Bowie Predicts the Impact of the Internet." Interview by Jeremy Paxman. BBC, 1999. Available at https://www.youtube.com/watch?v=FiK7s_0tGsg.

63. Rolling Stone. "David Bowie's 1999 Internet Prediction." January 11, 2016. https://www.rollingstone.com/music.

64. *Live Aid* Official Website. "Live Aid Lineup 1985." Accessed July 10, 2025. https://www.liveaid.fandom.com.

65. *Madison Blues*, composed by Elmore James and performed by George Thorogood and The Destroyers accompanied by Albert Collins.

66. *George Thorogood and the Destroyers: Live Aid Performance*, Philadelphia, 1985. *Live Aid Archive Video*, accessed July 10, 2025. https://www.youtube.com/watch?v=c4zCzYsyJZQ.

67. Bradberry, Travis. "Catalyst Leadership: Inspiring Change and Growth." *Harvard Business Review*, May 12, 2019.

68. Kotter, John P. *Leading Change*. Boston: Harvard Business School Press, 1996.

69. A Flock of Seagulls, *I Ran (So Far Away)*, released July 1982, Jive Records.

70. *Bands Reunited*, season 1, episode "A Flock of Seagulls," directed by Han Kim, aired February 2004, VH1.

71. Motörhead, *Overkill*, released March 24, 1979, Bronze Records.

72. "Interview with 'Fast' Eddie Clarke," *Classic Rock Magazine*, issue 128 (2009).

73. Dio, Ronnie James. Interview in A *Metalhead's Journey*. "Ronnie James Dio explains the malocchio / metal horns story." YouTube video: https://www.youtube.com/watch?v=Zai16APm3Ps

74. Jon Wiederhorn, "How Ronnie James Dio Made the Devil Horns Metal's Most Iconic Hand Gesture," *Loudwire*, May 16, 2017.

75. "Interview with Jimi Hendrix," *Rock & Folk Magazine*, December 1969, reprinted in *Classic Rock Interviews*, ed. Paul Du Noyer (London: Pan Books, 1994).

76. LinkedIn Corporation. "Types of LinkedIn Connections." *LinkedIn Help Center*. Accessed November 10, 2025. https://www.linkedin.com/help/linkedin.

77. Numan, Gary. Interview by The Vinyl Guide Podcast. *The Gary Numan Interview – The Vinyl Guide Podcast, Episode 284*. YouTube video, discussing the Minimoog story in the last chapter. Published on YouTube: https://www.youtube.com/watch?v=PGsoEQqbRhgg

78. Numan, Gary. *"Are 'Friends' Electric?"* Performed by Tubeway Army. Written by Gary Numan. Released May 1979. Beggars Banquet Records.

79. *Cars* written and produced by Gary Numan and performed by Gary Numan and his band. The song was released on August 24, 1979 and issued by the Beggars Banquet record label.

ABOUT THE AUTHOR

Shane grew up in Dublin, Ireland, where he attended Terenure College (High School). He qualified as a Chartered Accountant with Price Waterhouse Dublin and moved to New York in 1993.

A Fellow of Chartered Accountants Ireland, he also holds a master's in business administration from the Leonard N. Stern School of Business at New York University.

Shane spent many years in Internal Audit at CS First Boston and Credit Suisse, where he also held management positions in E-Commerce, Strategic Projects, and Fixed Income Client Strategy. He later served as Managing Director and Chief Auditor Americas at Swiss Reinsurance Group for over a decade. Shane is an Risk Executive in a global insurance company.

He is currently Board President of Chartered Accountants Worldwide – Network USA, a volunteer role supporting the delivery of educational, professional, and networking services to Chartered Accountants across the US, Canada, and the Caribbean.

Shane has a lifelong passion for all things Internal Audit. He has presented at The Institute of Internal Auditors (IIA) Great Audit Minds (GAM) Conference 2023, The Future of Internal Audit, and at the IIA Emerging Leaders Conference 2023 – The Secret Weapon of Great Internal Auditors: Sales Skills. He has also published numerous articles on Internal Audit and risk topics, on LinkedIn.

Audit Conclusion	**Ratings Result**
This should outline the key issues raised in the audit. For brevity, it is best to write each weakness in the negative. We used a rubric as follows [Who (which function or team), has not done what]. Also, give credit to management for any key issues they self-identified pre-audit, as the overall audit result should be a blend of management self-identified points and Internal Audit issues.	Control environment rating Residual risk rating Show a matrix reflecting the audit rating result, typically a control rating, a residual risk or materiality rating. Inherent risk rating should be provided for reference.
Management Self-Assessment	**Key Risks covered within the audit**
This section should outline whether Internal Audit assesses management self-assessment as being effective, partially effective or ineffective and the basis for Internal Audit's rating. Further, summarize management's self-assessment and any areas where they identified important weaknesses, or indeed failed to do so. Internal Audit should include a standard sentence on management agreement with the audit results and Internal Audit's view on the adequacy of the remediation actions planned. ***[For example, Management agrees with the audit results and ratings and Internal Audit agrees that the remediation actions planned are sufficient to address the risks identified]***	In this section, name the top 2/3 risks from your operational risk taxonomy covered by the audit.
Audit Scope	**Management Self-assessment Rating [Risk Culture rating}**
Outline the audit objectives and any key areas excluded. Also outline any reliance on data analytics or use of artificial intelligence tools. Cross-reference to the detailed audit objectives and management self-assessments included in the report appendix.	Rate as either: Effective, Partially Effective or Ineffective
Background	**Remediation completion date**
Outline pertinent support information covering function or business strategy, legal entities used for booking activities, financial performance or growth, risk profile, headcount and team location(s).	This section flags when the issues in the audit report are expected to be fully remediated.

Audit Report Summary Page Template [Report Name, Date] (Illustration 1)

Audit Objectives	Audit Sub-objectives	Management Self-assessment, including specific weaknesses self-identified	Management Self-ratings pre Audit	Internal Audit Ratings and issues (Ref #s) from the audit report
Objective 1	Sub-objectives	Written overview provided by management before audit testing starts. This assessment should be a candid assessment of the business risk and control environment pertinent to each audit objective. Management should outline any issues they have raised in the ERM system pre-audit, including reference numbers, issue details, action plans and due dates. Each objective should be supported by a paragraph or two describing key risks and how these risks are effectively controlled, and if there are key control weaknesses, or alternative control practices, these should be noted. Management's assessment should be open, honest and candid and the best way is to consider this as a written re-cap from management to the company CEO or Chairperson. It should be accurate and concise. This format increases management accountability and promotes a transparent risk and control culture.	Management should rate their internal control environment using the corporate rating scale	Internal Audit should provide an independent rating for each objective using the same scale as management, reflecting both audit findings and management self-identified weaknesses. Wide variations in ratings outcomes between management and Internal Audit should prompt risk culture ratings or commentary.
Objective 2	Sub-objectives	As above	As above	As above
Objective 3	Sub-objectives	As above	As above	As above
Objective 4	Sub-objectives	As above	As above	As above

Internal Audit – Management Self-assessment Template (Illustration 2)

www.ingramcontent.com/pod-product-compliance
Lightning Source LLC
LaVergne TN
LVHW050909210926
848482LV00012B/382
* 9 7 9 8 9 9 4 9 0 9 8 0 5 *